The Essential Guide to
Aspergers Syndrome

Hilary Hawkes

Published in Great Britain in 2017 by
need2know
Remus House
Coltsfoot Drive
Peterborough
PE2 9BF
Telephone 01733 898103
www.need2knowbooks.co.uk

Contents

Chapter 9

Acknowledgements

Thank you to the parents of AS children, partners and AS adults who responded to my questionnaires and who shared their views and ideas.

Thank you also to the professionals who read individual chapters or the entire book and made very useful comments – especially to Maxine Aston (counsellor, supervisor, AS expert, author and national and international speaker at ASD conferences) for reading the chapter on AS and parenting. Thank you to autism/AS expert, trainer and author Sarah Hendrickx, of Hendrickx Associates, for reading the whole original manuscript (see help list for details).

Introduction

Asperger's syndrome (or AS) is a neurological developmental disorder on the autistic spectrum. It is an Autistic Spectrum Disorder or ASD. Unlike severe autism, AS on its own does not cause any impaired intellectual ability.

If you have AS, your disabilities or difficulties will lie in the areas of social skills, communication, relationships and social imagination. You may find it harder than others to understand the myriad of non-verbal clues that others take for granted. You may be less able to empathise naturally or to understand someone else's point of view.

You may have been accused of being unsympathetic, selfish and self-absorbed because of this difficulty. This is an unfortunate and upsetting misconception, given that you may well regard yourself as being generally fair, committed, honest, loyal, rational and dependable. And you probably are. The fact is, if you have AS then you literally think differently. There are aspects of life and the world that you will see in an entirely different way. You may find many aspects of life baffling, irrelevant, illogical and confusing.

You may have long suspected that you think differently about things – especially emotional or relational issues. You may also have noticed that you have a heightened sensory awareness that not all others have. If you have recently discovered that you have AS yourself, or if you are a parent or partner whose loved one has been diagnosed or suspected of having this condition, it is important to understand these neurological differences and why they occur.

Understanding a condition is the first step to living with it or living with it alongside others. With understanding we can find better ways of reacting, behaving and reaching full potential – whether this is in regard to a parent/child relationship, an intimate long term adult relationship or just understanding ourselves better.

This book is meant to be a consoling, understanding, informative and useful introductory/basic guide for anyone affected by AS, including:

- Parents discovering their child's AS.
- Couples affected by one of them having this condition.

- The adult with AS.

- Teachers needing a starting point for understanding and helping a child with AS in the school environment.

To most of the population, AS is an invisible condition. It is often overlooked by parents, employers, teachers, professionals and even those affected themselves. There may have been a feeling that something was not quite right, that something was missing. If, like the author, you have family members affected by ASDs, you may have noticed particular behaviours, disinterest in others or obsessive behaviour. In the case of a child, you may have been told that difficulties were due to developmental delay, dyslexia or extreme shyness.

You may not have AS yourself but, live with a husband/wife/partner who does. As a consequence of this, you may feel that you do not really connect on an emotional level or that your partner shows little empathy or real interest in you as a person. If you are an adult with AS, perhaps you have become depressed or anxious about your apparent differences and difficulties with relationships and other aspects of life. Eventually, realisation point is reached. The problem is diagnosed AS.

This book can be seen as a first and helpful step along the journey of discovering what such a diagnosis or realisation means. It addresses questions such as:

- How does a person 'get' AS?

- Will he/she grow out of it?

- How can communication and relationship difficulties be eased?

- How can a child with AS reach their full potential?

- Given that the divorce rate of such relationships where one has the disorder and one doesn't is so high (one Dutch estimate is 80% – as reported by the US organisation Aspires; not to be confused with the East Sussex organisation Aspire), can marriages and long term relationships really survive – and how?

- Where can you get real understanding and support?

- How can our lives be better?

This book does not pretend that living with someone who has the condition is easy. Nor does it underestimate the pain and struggle that many go through in their quest to live with this invisible disability. Many of the strategies for dealing with problems are suggested by those who have the inside insight, because they are affected by the disorder themselves.

Sharing self-help ideas is just that: a sharing of ideas. Some may help others, some may not. The aim of this book is to help you understand more about AS and to consider some of the possible ways of finding support and living with the condition.

Note for 2017 edition

In 2013 the American Psychiatric Association's Diagnostic and Statistical Manual of Mental Disorders, 5th edition (DSM-5), placed Asperger's Syndrome under theumbrella term Autism Spectrum Disorder. It was previously a separate disorder within the spectrum. For simplicity this book retains the term Asperger's Syndrome (or AS) for this part of the spectrum as it remains a name in use.

Disclaimer

This book is primarily a collection of research and the author advises that she does not claim medical qualifications. Anyone with concerns about Asperger's syndrome should consult their GP or healthcare professional for individual medical advice. Following programmes of treatment or taking medication should only be done under the advice and supervision of a medical or mental health professional.

The terms 'autistic' or 'AS' child/adult/person may be used for clarity and simplicity and do not intend to define an individual.

1

What is Asperger's Syndrome?

Let's begin by finding out exactly what AS is – or even what it isn't. And who started this Asperger's disorder stuff anyway? Had anyone even heard of it 20 years ago?

The amount of information out there about AS just keeps growing. There are various websites publishing detailed academic and scientific research findings if we are that way inclined and the National Autistic Society (NAS) has a wealth of information to inform and support us. We discover that AS is the preferred abbreviation for the syndrome while anyone who does not have AS is NT (that's neuro-typical). This implies, correctly, that NT people are more prevalent than AS people. Some experts say that about one in every 100 people are affected by AS (Maxine Aston).

History

Asperger's syndrome is named after Hans Asperger, the Austrian physician who spotted a certain set of characteristics.

In 1911, a psychiatrist called Eugen Bleuler used the word 'autistic' to describe the social isolation of his schizophrenic patients. 'Auto' is Greek for 'self', so it seemed a fitting word. ('Understanding and Treating Autistic Behaviours', *Part 1 Non-pharmacologic Therapy*, Vol No 32:11 – see sources of further information.)

In the 1940s, Leo Kanner published reports on autism. He had noticed an unusual pattern of behaviour in some children who came to his clinic – they engaged in strange repetitive routines, had problems with language, were often mute and were unable to connect with others. Kanner called the condition early infantile autism.

In 1944, an Austrian paediatrician called Hans Asperger (1906-80) described a pattern of behaviour and certain characteristics in some of the children in his clinic. He felt, though, that these children would grow up to be exceptional individuals in the areas of work they chose.

However, while they were gifted intellectually, he noticed that they had marked difficulties with social integration. They seemed unable to understand non-verbal clues, showed little or no interest in others and were physically clumsy to varying extents. Asperger called his young patients 'Little Professors' and published a paper about them in Germany. At the time he called the condition autistic psychopathy, with social isolation being the main feature. ('Understanding and Treating Autistic Behaviours', *Part 1 Non-pharmacologic Therapy,* Vol No 32:11 – see sources of further information.)

So that's where the word 'Asperger' comes from – another condition named after a doctor who spotted a certain set of characteristics. Kanner's name became linked with more profoundly affected autistic people, i.e. Kanner's autism.

From the 1980s onwards, other professionals in other parts of the world began researching and publishing papers about similar children, and eventually a set of diagnostic criteria was devised.

One of these professionals was Lorna Wing. A consultant psychiatrist with an autistic daughter, Lorna was one of the founders of the National Autistic Society in 1962. She preferred the name Asperger's syndrome to autistic psychopathy, and it was in 1992 that Asperger's syndrome was included in the World Health Organisation's *International Classification of Diseases*. Two years later it was added to the fourth edition of the *Diagnostic and Statistical Manual of Mental Disorders* (the American Psychiatric Association's reference book – otherwise known amongst professionals as the DSM-IV).

The triad of impairments

Lorna Wing believed there were three areas of disability experienced by those affected by ASDs. These three areas became known as the triad of impairments and are:

- Social interaction.
- Social communication skills.
- Social imagination.

Modern day definition

Today certain areas are examined and assessed in an individual to determine whether they have Autism Spectrum Disorder. It is also realised that not all people with AS have high academic or intellectual abilities and that AS can be found in people with average intelligence as well.

The features that are a guide relate to a lacking in the following:

- Social interaction shown by impairment in non-verbal behaviours (like eye contact, gesturing, etc).
- Development of peer relationships.

- Unprompted or spontaneous sharing.
- Social and emotional reciprocity.

Restrictive interests and repetitive behaviours are also features. Today AS is described as a developmental disorder on the autistic spectrum and is at the higher functioning end of the spectrum. It is a life-long, hidden disability that affects different individuals in different ways.

Characteristics of AS

Every individual with AS is different and may exhibit different characteristics of the disorder. Any one person may not have all the difficulties and any one person may have more difficulties in one area than another person with AS. The main characteristics that have been found in those diagnosed with AS are as follows:

Every individual with AS is different and may exhibit different characteristics of the disorder.

Social communication problems

- Finding non-verbal communication from another person difficult to pick up or interpret. For example, not or not always understanding facial expression, not recognising clues for starting or ending a conversation, taking phrases very literally and having difficulty understanding jokes.

Social interaction problems

- Finding it hard to make close friendships or even feeling the need for close relationships. Not showing much interest or showing no interest in other people's points of view, interests or needs. Being unaware that others have emotional needs or, indeed, being unaware of what emotional needs are.

Social imagination problems

Imagination in this sense does not refer to the creativeness of a person – many people with AS are successful authors, artists, etc. Social imagination refers to the ability to pick up on the thoughts and feelings of others in order to react and respond appropriately.

- The subtle messages that we convey to each other via facial expression, posture, tone of voice, etc may be difficult to understand if you have AS. You may either ignore them or just be confused by them.

- Children with AS may find it hard to play imaginative games as it is difficult for them to put themselves in the place of an imaginary character and behave accordingly. This is because it is hard for them to work out how such a person would behave.

Other characteristics

Mindblindness and theory of mind

Human beings are able to mindread – it is a developmental skill acquired in childhood. We mindread when we work out what someone means or intends by observing emotions, words and behaviours of others. People use visual clues like facial expressions, body language and tone of voice, as well as listening to what that person is saying. When someone is unable to mindread, it is known as mindblindness. Many experts believe that autism is a kind of mindblindness.

Doctor and researcher Simon Baron-Cohen describes this more fully in his book *Mindblindness: An Essay on Autism and Theory of Mind* (see book list). Baron-Cohen believes that those on the autistic spectrum have mindreading impairment.

Some experts believe that brain imaging studies reinforce this theory of mindblindness. This is because in research experiments the brains of non-AS volunteers showed which parts of the brain are at work during mindreading. Scans of volunteers with an ASD showed the suggestion of weak connections between the different parts of the brain when engaged in activities that required the skill of mindreading. Similar impairment of mindreading or mentalising was found in subjects who had brain lesions or had undergone specific area brain surgery. See sources of further information of more details.

Many experts believe autism is a kind of mindblindness.

Routines and obsessions

As a sufferer of AS, you might find that you prefer routines and sameness. Always doing things the same way, having things in the same order and working to the same timetable can feel both reassuring and logical. Forced changes may be stressful for you and you may become very upset and angry when unnecessary changes are made to your environment or routines.

Some people with AS also have obsessive compulsive disorder (OCD), which is not the same as a need for routine and order. OCD is an anxiety disorder and it might show itself as checking, ritualistic hand washing, ruminating, etc. OCD is explained more fully in chapters 4 and 7.

Language and hearing

Having an excellent grasp of language and being highly articulate is often regarded as a good characteristic of AS. However, difficulties with hearing or speaking may include problems with auditory discrimination, literal interpretation of what someone else has said, pedantic responses, vocalising thoughts (known as echolalia) and unusual rhythm of speech or tone.

Sensory problems

People with AS can have sensory difficulties related to noise, touch, temperature, sight, smell and taste. The difficulty may be that the particular sense is either over-developed or under-developed. For example, an intolerance of the texture of certain foods, the feel of certain fabrics against the skin, the smell of perfumes or other cosmetics, etc.

Many people with AS find crowded places difficult to cope with – the noise, jostling and general navigational skills required can be difficult and painful when you are experiencing sensory overload.

Motor and co-ordination problems

Some people with AS have difficulties with movement or co-ordination. This may range from being unable to co-ordinate hand and arm movements to catch a ball, an odd gait when walking, to poor handwriting and difficulties with balance. Others may have actual movement disorders such as Tourette's syndrome.

Stimming

Stimming is a self-stimulatory repetitive action which looks like a habit or tic. Some of the most noticeable are vocal or visual – they might be grunting or throat clearing sounds or repetitive rapid eye-blinking, sniffing, rocking or hand flapping. Whatever they are, whatever they look like, their purpose is to provide a pleasurable self-stimulatory or calming sensation. We all have habits and behaviours that have calming effects for us. The difference in people with an ASD is that they can be far more unusual, persistent or noticeable – and they are more important to them.

Co-morbid conditions

Co-morbid conditions are those that exist alongside the main one, e.g. someone with AS may also have OCD. Some other co-morbid conditions experienced by people with AS include: attention deficit disorder (ADD), attention deficit hyperactivity disorder (ADHD), dyslexia, dyspraxia, hearing or visual impairments, language disorders, Tourette's syndrome and psychiatric disorders.

Visual thinkers

It is often cited that most people with AS (but not all) have a mainly visual way of thinking. Many experts back up this theory and say that it explains why many individuals with AS excel at chess, snooker, science, etc. If you have AS, you may have noticed, or perhaps others have pointed out, that you have a good eye for detail. This can mean you spot tiny details in things or that you can produce detailed and accurate work if you are artistic and creative. Unfortunately, much school and educational work is based on a verbal style of learning, so problems can arise for the AS student if their preferred learning style is not taken into account.

Not seeing the big picture

This means seeing and attaching significance to specific details in a situation rather than paying attention to the significance of the whole matter. For example, your child with AS may note that the driver of the last bus you have both just missed is the same driver of the bus you went on earlier. They may pay more attention to that than the main concern in the situation – that you will now have to walk home.

Specialist subjects

This will be a subject, hobby or pastime of intense and special interest to the person with AS. If you have AS, the chances of you having a subject or hobby at which you have developed, or would like to develop, a high level of skill or talent is very likely. Sometimes such an interest can develop into a life-long career, job, or interest. More often the interest will be of an intellectual and solitary nature, involving intense mental concentration and effort.

The good things

If you have a brain that works in the AS way, you may have found that this often gives you a considerable advantage when it comes to intellectual achievement. Having a higher than average IQ, or at least being of average ability, is a feature of the condition.

Some people with AS are high achievers in their areas of interest. When this is combined with a high level of commitment and an ability to focus and work consistently and accurately, great results can be achieved.

If you have AS, you may have noticed that you have an ability to focus easily for long lengths of time on tasks that interest and absorb you. You are lucky indeed! Some people without AS find emotional distractions can prevent this focus and absorption – so having AS is a considerable advantage in this respect.

If your partner has AS, you might feel that he/she exhibits a great deal of loyalty and commitment to your relationship. Whatever your situation, having AS is not something to be ashamed of. The talents and qualities of individuals with this condition can outweigh the social disabilities.

Some people with AS are high achievers in their areas of interest.

How does a person 'get' AS?

AS, as a form of autism and a developmental condition, affects the way the brain processes information. According to the National Autistic Society (NAS), research suggests that AS is caused by a combination of genetic and environmental factors which affect brain development (NAS 'What is Asperger Syndrome' leaflet).

The exact causes are still being investigated, but recent research has seen interesting breakthroughs in identifying a particular genes, and a particular gene which appears 'switched off' in those with ASDs.

In the world of autism research there is some hope that one day ways may be found to 'switch on' the disabled gene – thus enabling the brain to respond and develop in a neuro-typical rather than autistic manner. This might be achieved with the use of drugs or behavioural training from a very early age. That might be regarded as a cure. (MIT News, Feb 17, 2016: Neuro scientists reverse autism symptoms).

However, many experts and adults with AS argue that no 'cure' is needed. There are interventions that enable an affected person to live and lead as full a life as is possible.

Summing Up

AS is a developmental, relational disorder that is believed to affect one in 100 people. It is characterised by particular areas of impairment which are caused by neurological differences in the make-up of the brain.

While individual personality, upbringing, experiences and interests all bear a part in determining how we appear to others and how we relate to others, if you have AS you will tend to exhibit features common to the condition. These may include obsessive behaviour, degrees of difficulty with reciprocity and empathy and difficulty with communication.

Finding out what AS actually is, and the many ways it manifests or characterises those who have it, is the first step you need to take to understand the condition – whether you suffer from it yourself or live with someone who does.

Once you understand what AS actually is and realise the problems it may be causing are not anyone's fault, you may find you can develop a new understanding and perspective that can help you make changes to benefit you and your relationship.

- Visit the National Autistic Society's (NAS) website for further information and consider becoming a member.

- Obtain and read at least one textbook that gives more detail about ASDs. See the book list for ideas.

- Find out (possibly from the NAS) if there are any support groups for adults or children with AS or their families/partners in your area.

2

Recent Research

The information in this chapter provides a very basic overview of some of the areas of research going on into ASDs. For detailed information on these and other research projects, you should access official documentation or publications produced by the experts in these individual areas.

A purpose for research

Research offers the hope that new and improved methods may be found for helping those affected by ASDs. More than that, the research findings should teach us that those labelled as having autism or AS have very real neurological differences that explain certain behaviours. Where these behaviours are disabling, they should be shown tolerance and acceptance in society.

Alarmingly, it used to be thought that ASDs were the result of bad parenting, although scientific evidence was not found to support this view. Today scientists know there are significant differences in the workings of the brain in people with ASDs. Findings by researchers also show that within families there is very often a range of developmental delays or autistic type features or disabilities. Consequently, this has led to genetic research.

Today scientists know there are significant differences in the workings of the brain in people with ASDs.

How many people in the UK have AS?

According to the National Autistic Society, the estimate for people with some form of autism in the UK is around 700,000, with more males than females diagnosed. That's more than one in every 100 people. See www.autism.org.uk, 'Some facts and statistics'.

Although these figures are for all types of ASDs, expert Maxine Aston states that about one in every 100 also applies to those who have just AS (see www.maxineaston.co.uk). It may be that the true AS figure is hidden because many such people lead successful and fulfilling lives and are therefore not noticed for having the condition.

The National Autistic Society also states that the majority of people with ASDs are male. Ratios range from 2:1 to 16:1.

Types of research

Genetic research and gene therapy

There is much investigation and research into looking at what genes are responsible for causing autism. Different approaches have been devised to locate these problem genes and to look at how these genes might be altered through behavioural therapy.

The work of Dr Christopher Walsh and his team shows some interesting results in this area of research. Some of Dr Walsh's findings are published online. See sources of further information for details.

In Cambridge, the Autism Research Centre (ARC) is carrying out other interesting research projects, including the 'Whole Genome Study of Asperger's Syndrome' and research into perception, cognition, hormones and development in toddlers and sibling toddlers.

Research has also looked at the effect of testosterone in amniotic fluid and the later emergence of autistic traits in the baby. This finding has given rise to discussion about whether in the future it will be possible to develop prenatal screening for autism so that diagnosis could be made before birth and parents could be better prepared. The ARC website has further details of these research areas (see help list).

Other research programmes are looking into the idea that in the future there will be ways to 'switch on' the currently 'switched off' genes that are often partly responsible for some autism. See www.autismresearch.com.

MEG scanners work by measuring the tiny magnetic fields generated by the brain's activity.

Brain scanners

Special brain scanners are used to enable doctors and researchers to study the brains of people as they take part in thinking activities. MEG scanners and other scanners like MEG (MEG stands for magneto encephalography which means magnetic brain record) work by measuring the tiny magnetic fields generated by the brain's activity.

As well as showing how the brain's workings differ in those with ASDs, scanning can also enable the study of other neurodevelopment conditions. The subject sits upright and partly enclosed in the scanner, which slightly resembles a rather large chair. The scanner then uses a technique that detects the minute magnetic fields generated by brain electrical activity.

Areas studied or being studied with MEG include:

- Face processing.

- Semantic (language) processing.

- Choice making.

Behavioural intervention research

Behavioural intervention research is looking at ways that different interventions can help develop impaired skill areas in those with ASDs. For example, developing computer based games that can help autistic people develop or improve social skills.

Over the years, various views have developed as to how to alleviate some of the difficulties people with AS experience. As AS is not an illness, these programmes cannot really be called treatments – really they are more like behavioural therapies that will help improve the individual's life. The interventions tend to concentrate on key areas of difficulties that AS people experience – developing communication skills, dealing with obsessions and physical motor co-ordination. The earlier the intervention, the better.

For many years, different treatment or therapy programmes have existed that help and enhance the behaviour and development of more severely affected autistic children. These programmes can also help children with AS (as a less severe form of autism). Such programmes include TEACCH (Treatment and Education of Autistic and Communication Handicapped Children).

The main long term goal of TEACCH is to encourage skills and personal development in autistic children. Children are helped to understand the world around them, to communicate and relate to others and to learn how to make choices and decisions for themselves. Constant assessment of achievement and potential is used to base the frequently revised and updated therapy programme. These assessments are called PEP or psych educational profile.

When undesirable behaviour arises, the underlying reasons are looked at, i.e. anxiety, boredom, loss of routine, etc. TEACCH works on these underlying conditions to enable further learning to occur. More information about TEACCH can be found on the National Autistic Society's website.

The PLAY project is another therapy intervention programme. Developed by Dr Richard Solomon, the aim of PLAY (Play and Language for Autistic Youngsters) is to show parents how to become their child's play partner, enabling a child who was once remote and distant to engage and enjoy some kind of social interaction.

The basic idea is to start by echoing or joining in whatever behaviour your child is showing and then to move this onto further desirable activity or behaviour. Parents or carers learn the methods from trained practitioners. A training DVD and further information is available from the PLAY project website at www.playproject.org.

Social skills programmes

There are also social skills training programmes for children and young adults with AS. These can be effective in helping young people cope with social interaction. The groups work best when they provide structured activities and are consistent in reinforcing desired behaviour.

Further information on finding out more about these and many other interventions is included in chapter 4 and the help list.

Drugs

To date, no medication has been invented that can 'cure' ASDs. On the advice and under the supervision of qualified medical practitioners, medication can be and is often prescribed to support those who need to control anxiety, depression, anger or obsessive tendencies.

Prevalence

Some researchers are interested in why there appears to be increased numbers of people being diagnosed with ASDs. Some believe this is due to increased knowledge and awareness of these conditions and others are looking into possible environmental causes.

There are also social skills training programmes for children and young adults with AS. These can be effective in helping young people cope with social interaction.

Some researchers have noticed pockets of increased prevalence of ASDs and are looking into the interesting theory of whether this could be due to high numbers of scientific minded people working in these areas, meeting each other and in time producing children who inherit these autism prone genes. This theory is discussed by researcher Steve Silberman in his article, 'The Geek Syndrome', currently viewable online – see sources of further information for details.

Less autism in the future?

In time, perhaps medical and scientific research will discover ways to prevent or cure ASDs. Discovering interventions and treatments that enable individuals to lead their lives to the full are good. However, would we want to have a world that is without the unique and special contributions that some people with ASDs offer?

Where would we be without the contributions of Bill Gates, Michael Palin, Alfred Hitchcock, Isaac Newton, Jane Austen, Albert Einstein, Henry Cavendish, Charles Darwin, Satoshi Tajriri, Jim Henson, Charles Salz, Thomas Jefferson, Michelangelo, Wolfgang Mozart, George Orwell, Dan Aykroyd, Ludwig Van Beethoven, Thomas Eddison and Woody Allen? All these individuals have or are believed to have had AS. See www.asperger-syndrome.me.uk for details.

Summing Up

Some of the main research areas are in the fields of genetics, brain development before birth, brain scanning and behavioural interventions. By looking at some of the research that is going on into the possible causes of ASDs, you can start to understand what a diagnosis of AS is – whether it's for yourself, your partner or your child. There are many books that explore research into autism in detail. World autism expert Professor Simon Baron Cohen's are particularly good.

3

Diagnosing AS

The benefits of diagnosis

If you are the parent of a child suspected of having AS, you've probably been through many turbulent years of wondering what it is about your child that is not quite right. Your child may already have had paediatric tests and assessments for other disorders due to concerns from a teacher, health visitor, GP or yourself.

The concern that AS is the cause of your child's difficulties may have come about when they were being treated for a related condition – e.g. ADHD, OCD or dyslexia. Maybe the professionals felt that even though these disorders were present, it wasn't the full story.

If you think you have AS or live with someone who may have it, you may feel that you would gain great relief and reassurance from finding out. Knowing for sure means that you can stop blaming all manner of things for the difficulties. If you're a parent, you'll know that it is not your parenting skills at fault. You can access help and support for your child at school. You can discover interventions that may support your child as he/she grows up. If you're an adult suspecting you have AS, a diagnosis will explain the differences and specific difficulties you have. It can be reassuring to know there is a reason. If your partner has AS then you can learn strategies and find the right kind of support that will help you both to understand and strengthen your relationship.

There are those who choose not to know for sure. They feel the label of a particular disorder is more of a disadvantage than an advantage and that individuality and individuals reaching their full potential is all that matters. However, today there is growing awareness of the specific needs and the very special contribution of individuals with ASDs, and having a diagnosis of AS should never be regarded as a stigma.

If you are finding it difficult to decide whether or not to pursue a diagnosis for yourself, you may like to consider the following:

- Would knowing help you to understand yourself better?

- Would it help those closest to you to understand your difficulties better, leading to greater tolerance and support where required?

- Would it enable access to needed services, benefits or employment advice?

If you have other worries or questions, contact the National Autistic Society helpline – see help list for details.

When you think your partner has AS

If you live in an intimate relationship with someone whom you suspect has AS, how can you go about suggesting this to them? When talking to someone about the possibility of them having AS, you could consider the following:

- Choose a time when you can be undisturbed and when you know your partner is stress-free.

- Find a suitable way to approach the subject – you could say that you have read something about AS or someone else you know has AS.

- If it was something you read, have a copy to hand.

- One of the National Autistic Society leaflets explaining what AS is might be useful to show your partner.

- Respect whatever reaction you get. Possible reactions could be annoyance, anger, interest, denial or relief.

- Tell your partner why you have mentioned this – that it would be important for you both to know if one of you has AS.

- Away from your partner, find someone – a friend, family member or other supportive person – to talk to about your suspicions. Your AS partner will not be able to empathise with any distress you feel. At what can be a difficult and emotionally turbulent time, you will need to find someone to help you come to terms with this realisation. Having this support will be even more essential for you if your partner is later diagnosed with the condition.

- If you get a very negative reaction, try asking your partner to read the literature you have on AS. If your partner does have it, they might well recognise this in themselves if given time to take in the information.

Diagnosis

Who can diagnose?

Suitably qualified mental health professionals can carry out diagnostic procedures that lead to an official diagnosis of AS. These professionals include psychiatrists, clinical psychologists or, in the case of children, paediatricians.

There are two main routes to accessing these people. You may wish to take the NHS route which would involve going to your GP and asking for a referral to a diagnostician with experience in the field of autism. Alternatively, you may wish to take the private route. If following this route, you will need to contact the diagnostician yourself.

The National Autistic Society has a small directory of suitably qualified and experienced practitioners and this can be accessed through their website contact/enquiries system – see help list for details.

In some cases, you may already be in the mental health system, e.g. if you are the parent of a child having support for other issues from CAMHS (the National Health Service's Child and Adolescent Mental Health Services for those up to age 18). Or, if it is you, the adult, you may already be seeing a mental health professional about other issues. If these professionals suspect AS then they can make the referral to the diagnostician for you, assuming they cannot do the diagnosing themselves.

Some psychologists and counsellors are very experienced in the area of working with and supporting those affected by AS. Some may be able to carry out assessments that can indicate whether someone has AS and whether, if done, a formal diagnosis would be likely.

You may be an adult who prefers not to have the formal diagnosis for yourself. You may be happy with your own self-diagnosis or a psychologist's/counsellor's less formal assessment. You may find Professor Simon Baron-Cohen's Autism Quotient or AQ test useful. While this is not a formal diagnostic tool, it indicates where you may be on the autistic spectrum. Scores above a certain level are a very strong indication that any formal diagnostic test would be positive. At the time of writing, the test can be accessed online – visit www.autismresearchcentre.com and click on 'tests'. Or see AQ Test in the help list.

How long is the wait for a referral?

If you take the NHS route and there is no urgency, the wait for an appointment with the diagnostician can be some months. Many parents report that their child's diagnosis came after many years of being referred to one professional after another. This can happen when AS is not suspected immediately.

If you take the private route getting an appointment is much faster, but can be expensive.

Medical records

When a diagnosis is made, a record of this is usually kept in the person's medical records. The exception is when the diagnosis has been made by a private practitioner – while a full report is usually sent to the client/patient, it may not be sent to the GP as well. Some adults feel concerned that the mention of the disorder in their medical records may have a detrimental effect on their careers if medical references are ever required. These adults usually, therefore, take the private route for diagnosis.

How is a diagnosis made?

The main international diagnostic classification is either:

- The International Classification of Diseases, 10th edition, referred to as ICD-10 (World Health Organisation, 1992), or
- The Diagnostic and Statistical Manual of Mental Disorders, 5th edition, referred to as DSM-V (American Psychiatric Association, 2013).

These criteria consist of questions about different areas of development, ability and skills. The diagnostician will ask questions related to social and emotional abilities and responses, and communication, cognitive and movement skills.

In the case of a child, the parents will also be interviewed by the diagnostician and questions are asked about the child's all round development from birth. There will also be questions about how the child plays and relates to others. A teacher's report may also be useful. One such parent/carer questionnaire is known as the Autism Diagnostic Interview or ADI. ADI or ADI R (revised).

The diagnostician will then spend at least an hour with the child, asking questions and making observations from games and play situations which they will engineer. One such assessment is known as the Autism Diagnostic Observation Schedule or ADOS.

The whole diagnosis procedure will probably last several hours and may be done in more than one visit.

The diagnostician will ask questions related to social and emotional abilities and responses, and communication, cognitive and movement skills.

How easy is it to make the diagnosis?

Some mental health professionals feel that it is not at all easy, while others believe their experience enables them to recognise the condition quite quickly. Diagnosis has to be made by identifying behaviour patterns that have been present in the person to some extent from very early childhood, and some features can be present due to other conditions.

However, whatever system for diagnosis is used, it is generally agreed that where significant impairments of social interaction, communication and imagination are found, along with some obsessiveness for sameness and routine, then diagnosis can be made.

Preparing a child for the diagnosis

A child or young person may be quite fearful of being taken along to a clinical setting to be left (for some of the time) with a complete stranger who asks all manner of peculiar questions or who wants to play games.

It is a good idea to prepare your child for the appointment. As the child's parent, you will know what situations produce most anxiety and stress in your child. Not knowing what to expect or why they are going can lead to anxiety in itself.

If your child has already had assessments or tests for other possible disorders (dyslexia, dyspraxia, OCD, etc), they may already feel that everyone is thinking there is something wrong with them. You need to find a way to tell your child that everyone is different and that some people have differences that need special attention so they can find out how to overcome certain problems.

You could mention other people the child knows who have had tests and special treatment, e.g. someone who has eye tests and needs spectacles or someone with diabetes who needs to eat at certain times and has insulin. Explain that it is a good idea to find out if someone has something special about them so they can get the help they need. The idea is to normalise the purpose of the diagnosis as far as possible.

Most settings that diagnose children are used to employing methods that help children feel more comfortable, secure and at ease. Ideally there will be toys, colourful décor, a waiting area nearby for parents, toilets, etc. The qualified and experienced mental health professional will also know how to approach and talk to your child before and during the diagnostic testing.

What happens next?

By the end of the testing, the diagnostician will know if AS is the diagnosis and will probably tell you straightaway. Whether you expected a diagnosis of AS or not, you might still feel some shock and concern.

At some point you will be given the opportunity to ask questions and a report outlining the outcome of the test is usually sent to you and possibly to your GP. In the case of a child, you can pass a copy to the school. You may be given further information about AS and advice on where to go for further information, support services, counselling, etc.

Accepting the diagnosis and moving on from that point are dealt with in chapter 7 for an adult with AS, chapter 4 for parents of a child with AS and chapter 8 for the partner of someone with the diagnosis.

Explain that it is a good idea to find out if someone has something special about them so they can get the help they need.

Summing Up

Getting a firm diagnosis of AS can help you understand yourself and your difficulties better, and it can enable you to gain access to support and services. In the case of children, it will enable you to try various interventions that will help your child develop and reach their full potential.

4

The Child with AS

A lot of children are almost in their teens before they are diagnosed with AS. In some cases, this is because they appear to cope and function very well on certain levels. This can then mask the difficulties that stem from having what is often seen as a relational disorder (see glossary).

Who to tell

The diagnostician may already have told your child that they have AS (especially if the child is older). However, if you have been left to do this yourself, you will need to think of the best way of approaching this. Remember to get your child to think of all their strengths and abilities and to see the AS as a difference rather than a disability.

You will obviously need to inform your child's school, and having this information will help them support your child further. Whether you inform relatives, friends and neighbours is entirely up to you and your child. You may want to use a 'who needs to know' basis for disclosure.

The main thing is to ensure that those you do tell have a proper understanding of the condition. You can even obtain leaflets and books from the National Autistic Society to lend to those who want to know more.

Remember to get your child to think of all their strengths and abilities and to see the AS as a difference rather than a disability.

Reactions to the diagnosis

As a parent, you may react in different ways to the diagnosis. This is normal! Common reactions include:

- Relief.
- Disbelief.
- Fear for the future.

Relief can be due to finally feeling that at long last the professionals have listened, taken your concerns seriously and your child will now get the help and support needed.

Disbelief can be due to not really knowing what AS is. The term ASD can be a scary one if you are, as yet, unaware that the spectrum is a very wide one and that those at the high functioning end (those with AS or high functioning autism) generally lead full and normal lives.

It is natural to feel concerned about your child's future, but with the right help and encouragement there should be no reason why your child cannot grow into a mature, capable and responsible young adult. Armed with knowledge and support, you can help your child reach their full potential in the same way that all parents can with any child. Your child will have many strengths and abilities which can be nurtured and developed.

Depending on what led you to seek the diagnosis, your immediate concerns may now include the following areas:

- Your child's social skills and development.
- Communication problems.
- Tantrums.
- Sensory, obsessive and anxiety issues.
- The impact on other family members, including getting support for yourself.
- Your child's way of thinking and learning.
- Behaviour problems.
- Getting support at school.

(The last three points above are discussed in chapter 5).

Social skills

It can be upsetting to realise that your child has few or possibly no real friends. It can be even more upsetting when your child very evidently wants friendship but simply has no idea how to go about achieving this in the normal or natural way.

In order to understand why AS children find initiating and maintaining friendship a problem, it may be useful to look at how non-AS children (or anyone for that matter) manage this. It will then be possible to explain to your child how they can change their behaviour and approach to others. While this may not feel natural or spontaneous to them, social skills are something that can be taught and practised.

So how do non-AS children make and keep friendships?

Their natural techniques can include:

- Showing interest in others.

- Sharing ideas and accepting alternative ideas for play.

- Being aware that others may have feelings that sometimes differ from their own.

- Understanding codes of conduct.

- Recognising non-verbal clues.

Immediately we can see that these are all things that children with AS find difficult. They are not naturally aware of the feelings, intentions and emotions of others.

The following table shows how you can encourage your child to develop social skills and friendships. The ideas are suggestions from other parents of children with AS.

Social skills and friendships

Suggestion	Description	Benefits to your child
Special groups for children with AS	Accessed via CAHMS, these may run for a few weeks/months. Small groups are used for role play, talking, etc.	Teaches social skills. Allows children to work/play together in a safe environment, supervised by a professional who will understand the difficulties.
Parent workshops	Accessed via the National Autistic Society e.g. behavioural strategy workshops.	Gives parents a chance to share ideas, learn and develop skills that they can teach their child.
Help at school	Ask your child's teacher about any special small group activities that help children develop socially and emotionally. Can one be set up?	This particularly benefits children who might otherwise be isolated – creates a chance to participate in an adult initiated friendship/social group.
Hobbies	Encourage your child to develop their special interest(s) by joining clubs or societies for people with those same interests e.g. chess, swimming, etc.	Your child may make friends with those who share the same interests.
Playing with your child	Encourage your child to play games with you that involve negotiating, turn taking, etc. Show interest in and expand your child's special interest.	Helps children develop interaction skills – the to and fro of conversation, turn-taking, being flexible and spontaneous, etc. This will show your child that it is possible to enjoy someone else's 'world' or idea. You will be modelling the behaviour you want them to achieve i.e. showing interest in others.
Drama classes	Role play, acting, etc.	Develops confidence and self-esteem and enables children to examine the details of people's reactions, emotions or different situations.

Social Stories TM	These are therapeutic stories for social situations that give ideas for how to react, behave, etc. You could write your own to fit your child or obtain already published stories (see help list).	Helps your child think through how to behave or react in different situations. Can help relieve anxiety.
Specialist youth groups	Special youth groups for children with AS, e.g. Children in Touch in Oxfordshire.	Knowledgeable staff supervise the children/adolescents and encourage activities that promote self-esteem and social skills.
Invite friends	If your child is still young enough, you could invite friends around on his/her behalf to encourage the making of friendships. If your child finds this very difficult, supervise some structured activities.	Your child will meet others and have opportunities to develop friendships in the security of the home environment.
Special interventions e.g. TEACHH, ABA, Son-Rise	Investigate some of the intervention programmes for autistic children. These can also be beneficial for AS children.	Helps your child practise and develop interaction and social skills. See help list for details of which organisations give further details of these.

Talk about yourself, what you did today, how you felt and why. Talk about other people in the same way.

Other tips for helping your child

- Teach your child the difference between honesty and rudeness. When they make mistakes within the family, point them out and explain how what was said would have been interpreted.

- If your child is going into a new or strange situation, go through what might happen, what they could say and what they should do.

- Talk about yourself, what you did today, how you felt and why. Talk about other people in the same way.

Whatever strategies you use to help your child, remember that they are an individual whose nature and personality must be respected. You cannot force a child who prefers their own company to become more sociable. Too much force and your well meaning efforts may backfire.

The aim is to teach the young person with AS how to interact, understand and relate to others as best they can. You can encourage a child who feels lonely and would like friends to explore ways of achieving those friendships. Many children with AS desperately want friends and to feel part of the class or group and just need to be shown ways to do this without feeling uncomfortable or anxious.

Communication

Communication and language problems for a child with AS may be in any or all of these areas:

- Not knowing how to start or keep a conversation going.
- Taking things literally.
- Always using pedantic speech.
- Vocalising thoughts and echolalia.
- Not speaking with fluency and prosody.

The art of conversation

The art of conversation can be a bit of a mystery to children (and adults for that matter) who have AS. How do people know when to start talking, when to join in without actually interrupting and when to stop? How do people keep conversations going? How do people know when others are bored by what they are saying?

Practice might not make perfect here but, it will certainly go a long way to helping your child learn about the skills of talking to others.

A lot of the answers are down to the non-verbal clues we pass each other as we speak and listen, so a child with AS is obviously going to miss out on keeping up with and interpreting these signals. Practice might not make perfect here, but it will certainly go a long way to helping the child learn about the skills of talking to others.

Your child will become familiar with these skills when you:

- Encourage them to tell you about their day.
- Share your own news with them.
- Encourage them to ask other people questions about themselves or what they've done.
- Pause and wait for the response after you have asked your child a question.

- Show interest when they talk endlessly about their special interest(s) – but make sure you expand and try to lead the conversation onto other topics.

Literal interpretation

Your child with AS may have a tendency to interpret speech literally, causing them great difficulty with metaphorical phrases and jokes. There are two things you can do here:

- Avoid metaphorical speech as much as possible. If you do use it, explain what it really means.

- Look up the origins and meanings of sayings together. That way your child will quickly learn that people don't always mean what they say!

Your child may make other less obvious mistakes in interpretation and this can easily happen at school too. For example, a teacher who says 'It's very cold in the playground today' may expect an AS child to know that the hidden instruction here is 'get your coat from the peg and put it on before you go out'. At home we can learn to express and explain in appropriate ways, but others in contact with your child may not have this insight, so you will need to help them.

Pedantic speech

This is where the child insists that everything you say is literally correct.

You may feel that your child is forever correcting your words or making strange comments that strangle the meaning or emotion behind what you have just shared.

Below are some real examples (and you will probably have many others):

Parent: 'Do you think you are going to enjoy that book?'

Child: 'I don't know. How can I know if it's going to be enjoyable until I've read it?'

Parent: 'Please put those socks in the wash.'

Child: 'It's not the wash. It's called the washing machine.'

Parent: 'Isn't the park lovely today?'

Child: 'It's not any different to usual.'

The problem is that the child with AS finds ambiguity and uncertainty difficult to cope with and this can cause anxiety and stress. While it's important to use language that your child will understand, it is also useful to explain that people like to make comments and expect a pleasant and polite response in return. Don't give up making spontaneous comments to your child.

Talking to the self

Young children generally grow out of talking to themselves but the child with AS may continue this throughout childhood – or even through adulthood as well. They may be rehearsing what they will say or repeating pieces of conversation that have already taken place. The reasons for this could range from being a kind of companion to themselves to trying to make sense of something heard.

Other children who do not understand your child's need to do this might laugh or tease your child. If this becomes a problem, encourage your child to try talking to themselves in their head and not out loud.

Fluency and prosody

Children with AS can have an over formal and somewhat stilted way of speaking which can, at times, make understanding what they have said very difficult. While your child may have a good grasp of spoken vocabulary, their speech may not be that distinct.

You may find your child's speech varies even within the same conversation. It can start distinct and precise and then lose volume, pitch and tone, and you may need to ask your child to repeat the words. This could be a particular problem for boys reaching the stage when their voice deepens and changes.

Don't make a big issue of your child's speech or you may well make them anxious and self-conscious. If it is a very big problem then get professional advice and consider speech therapy.

Encourage your child to speak clearly and slowly. Don't make a big issue of your child's speech or you may well make them anxious and self-conscious. If it is a very big problem then get professional advice and consider speech therapy.

Tantrums

Children with AS often appear to over-react or throw tantrums. These are a bit more than the usual explosions of emotion exhibited by the average toddler or young child. Sometimes these angry outbursts are called 'melt downs' and older AS children and adults may also be prone to them.

Of course, we all have moments when we are unable to control our tempers. The difference with the AS child is that you will be able to see that they are having difficulty recognising signs of stress and frustration in themselves and they will be unable to control or deal effectively with these feelings.

When dealing with your AS child's tantrum, you may find the following points (suggested by other parents of AS children) useful:

- Learn to recognise the early warning signs that your child is becoming stressed or frustrated.

- Use distraction techniques if not too late – this might include suggesting an activity that enables your child to be alone for a short while.

- Do not wade in shouting and reprimanding your child. He/she will be unable to listen or rationalise what you are saying.

- Give your child some space and encourage others to do the same.

- Once the episode is over, insist that apologies are made where apologies are due and explain why if necessary.

- Your child may be puzzled that others remain stressed after the melt down moment has passed. AS children can recover quickly but you may need to explain why others are still feeling the effects of the outburst.

- On other occasions, talk to your child about emotions and why people react the way they do. Give examples of when things annoy or upset you and explain what you do to help yourself.

Do not wade in shouting and reprimanding your child. He/she will be unable to listen or rationalise what you are saying.

Sensory issues

Your AS child may be either over sensitive or under sensitive to certain stimuli and this may cause them particular difficulties. Over sensitiveness is very common in children (and adults) who have AS and may be related to things like noise levels, light brightness, the feel of certain fabrics, the taste or texture of certain foods or finding certain smells too strong or overpowering.

This over sensitiveness can show itself in the following ways: holding their hands over their ears in crowds, noisy environments or where several people are speaking at once; finding it difficult to cope outside in bright sunshine or to sit in direct sunlight in the car; eating a restricted diet; wearing clothing that seems inappropriate for the weather; disliking and maybe refusing to use perfumes, deodorants, etc.

Don't worry though – there are common sense strategies that will help your child manage their heightened senses, and together you can find ways of making most things tolerable or discover suitable and acceptable alternatives. Make sure that others – teachers, family and friends – understand that your child's intolerance is not due to being awkward but is part of the condition.

For some common sense strategies for dealing with sensory issues, visit the Sensory Processing Disorder Resource Centre online shop at www.sensory-processing-disorder.com.

Rigidity and routine

Adhering to rigid or strict routines is a common need of the child (or adult) with AS. They may find sudden changes of routine or changes to their environment difficult to cope with. Doing anything spontaneously can also cause great upset and disruption, unless it is their own idea.

Your child will probably (almost certainly) have a special interest and become absorbed in this for long lengths of time. While it is good that your child has an interest or hobby which develops his/her talents, interest and abilities, it is not good to become so obsessed that other experiences are missed. You may find yourself developing ways of controlling the length of time your child spends on their special interest so that other activities or people do not get overlooked. This is a particular issue when the special interest is computer games – as it very often is.

Your child will feel most secure and relaxed in the world of their special interest and, left to their own devices, would probably spend most of their time on this activity. Some parents use timetabling methods to encourage their AS child to do a greater variety of things. Others restrict the special interest to certain parts of the day, e.g. playing computer games in the morning or after homework only.

However, as long as your child does engage in other activities some of the time, their special interest may well, in time, prove to be a positive aspect of their life. Special interests often turn into the beginnings of future job interests and careers.

Some parents use timetabling methods to encourage their AS child to do a greater variety of activities.

Obsessive compulsive disorder (OCD)

Due to the high levels of stress experienced by children with AS, some children develop an anxiety disorder known as obsessive compulsive disorder or OCD.

OCD is not the same as ritualistic behaviour or a need for strict routine that is regarded as a common feature in those with ASDs. Instead, OCD is where a person engages in compulsive behaviour or habits to such an extent that they may, at the worst point, be unable to perform everyday tasks. Examples of such behaviours are persistent handwashing, checking things over and over again, being unable to walk through doorways without performing a particular ritual, being unable to eat certain foods and needing to touch things in a certain way or repeated manner.

OCD is a stressful condition both for the person who has it and for those who live with the sufferer. It is important to remember that it is more than a habit and needs to be properly recognised and treated. If you think your child has OCD, seek professional medical advice.

If you think your child has OCD, seek professional medical advice.

Non-AS individuals are often treated with medication (to lower anxiety levels) and cognitive behaviour therapy. Children (and adults) with AS may find treatment takes longer because of their difficulties with verbalising their thoughts and feelings, but it is important to get the right professional help

Support for the family and yourself

Siblings

It can be tough on the siblings of children who have AS as they may feel that the affected member of the family is getting more than their fair share of attention. You may find yourself spending endless amounts of time dealing with your AS child, leaving less energy and attention for your other children. If your AS child has significant behaviour problems, this will be even more the case.

If your other children are older, explain what AS is in more detail. This may help them to understand that any demanding problems their brother or sister has is not their fault. Teach your children that everyone is different, we all have different abilities and some people have particular difficulties. Be non-judgmental about this.

In your attempt to balance family relationships, you may like to consider the following points:

- While it is helpful to be flexible, do not allow AS to be an excuse for bad behaviour.

- Don't have double standards with regard to rules about behaviour – treat both/all your children the same as far as possible.

- Encourage your other children's interests and their own friendships.

- Have special times/outings for your non-AS children.

- Don't expect your non-AS children to be responsible for their AS brother or sister. It can be very common for siblings to worry about the future and who will care for their AS sibling (if they need caring for) once the parents are no longer alive.

- Let your non-AS children have space for themselves, e.g. their own room for their own possessions if possible.

- Encourage the caring attitude and insights your non-AS children may develop as a result of having a 'disabled' sibling.

- Let your non-AS children talk to you about AS. They may wonder if they have it themselves or worry if their own children in the future will have ASDs. Don't let inaccurate and scary fears develop in your children's minds because you have not given them the chance to voice their concerns.

- Don't underestimate the impact on siblings. Very common reactions for siblings include anxiety, depression, over-attachments (being too dependent on someone) and delinquent behaviour.

- Check the National Autistic Society's website for publications and helpful resources for siblings of children with AS.

- Check out Sibs at www.sibs.org.uk – this is the UK charity for siblings of disabled brothers and sisters.

Teach your children that everyone is different, we all have different abilities and some people have particular difficulties. Be non-judgmental about this.

You

You may at times feel overwhelmed with having to cope with your AS child's difficulties and behaviour, and it doesn't help that the majority of the population are still largely unaware of what AS is.

As an invisible disability, you might find yourself thinking you don't have anything to complain about and that if things are difficult then you just need to try harder. Invisible or not, any disability will place a strain on the family who has to live with the person who has it. As the child's parent or main carer, most of the burden will fall on you, and you will need support. If your partner also has AS then your need for ongoing support will be even greater as you will not receive the emotional support that couples can otherwise give each other.

Some parents of AS children find close friends and the wider family supportive and helpful. It may not always be a case of needing people who can occasionally give you time off or time to yourself, but more about having someone to talk to or somewhere to go to offload the stress and worries.

Counselling (see chapter 9) can help you find ways of managing your emotions and devising coping strategies for yourself. It is important to get professional medical advice if you feel over-stressed or depressed.

If you decide to try counselling, make sure you go to an appropriately qualified and registered counsellor. The British Association for Counselling and Psychotherapists (BACP) and the UK Council for Psychotherapy (UKCP) are two registering bodies for such counsellors, and the National Autistic Society has information about counsellors experienced in AS. There are also a number of private clinics that offer specialist counselling to families affected by AS. Those offered by Maxine Aston and Hendrickx Associates (see help list) are examples. Check with the National Autistic Society (see help list) for others or anything nearer to you.

Along with talking to other parents of AS children, I would like to suggest the following as ways that may help you keep a more balanced approach to life:

- Having your own interests away from family life.

- Developing your job or career.

- Keeping in regular touch with friends.

- Doing things you enjoy – having fun and laughing.

- Getting emotional support through friendships, having more time with your partner, counselling or other professional help.

- Meeting other parents in the same situation.

- Joining a support group for parents of children with AS.

Summing Up

Discovering that your child has AS and adjusting life to accommodate the difficulties your child has can be challenging and exhausting. Fortunately, there are many techniques that can help us find ways through many of the problems, whether at home or school.

Remember that your child has many abilities and qualities just like all other children. With the support and encouragement of the adults who influence them most, children with AS can develop these qualities and grow into happy and successful young adults.

Remember to take care of yourself and find sources of advice and support that work for you.

5

School and
the AS Child

This chapter looks at some of the possible problems a child with AS may have at school and how to deal with them.

Cognition and learning

Cognition means knowing and understanding. The sciences of cognitive psychology and of neurology offer suggestions and theories as to why a child with AS thinks and learns in a different way to a non-AS child.

Children with AS may show particular features in their approach to learning and understanding. These may include:

- Being at the extreme ends of the ability scale for different subjects.

- Perfectionism.

- Inability to apply learning from one situation to another. This is of significance for social behaviour too.

- Unusually good long term memory.

- Inability to mind read. This affects learning how to respond in social situations or in other learning where the child needs to explain the reactions of others, e.g. in studying literature, history, etc.

- Often a visual rather than a verbal style of learning which can result in the ability to remember minute and accurate detail.

The AS child and school

Some children with AS appear to achieve effortlessly in the academic areas of their education. Others find their different way of thinking and learning presents problems because it doesn't fit the teaching styles offered by the school. Some children with AS also have specific learning difficulties to contend with, causing further complications. While the majority of children with AS will manage in mainstream school, some need special support or even separate teaching in special units.

If your child is struggling at school, you will discover, if you haven't already done so, the special needs support system offered by the UK education system. The system of support is assessed and set up in different stages – depending on the level of learning difficulty discovered. However, if you and your child are already going down the route of getting special needs support, you will know it is often not as simple as that.

Find out from your child's school or your local authority how his/her educational needs can be assessed and supported. This process will differ depending on where in the UK you live. If your child is assessed as needing support there are different levels of help which are re-assessed at regular intervals as a young person moves through education.

If a child needs more support than a school or college can usually give, then an assessment for an Education Health and Care Plan will be made. A EHCP continues until the young person is 25 if still in education or training.

The Department for Education has easy read guides on support available on their website. Search SEND (special education needs and disabilities) on the Gov.UK website.

Homework

Again this is not an issue for some children with AS. Some manage to be motivated and have very few problems with getting homework done. For other AS children and their parents, such a scenario can only be a dream. From day one, homework presents unimaginable torture, stress and exhaustion – not only for the child but for the parent(s) as well. The amount of homework produced often does not reflect the amount of time spent trying to produce it or the intelligence level of the child.

Teachers may be unaware of this if the child appears to cope satisfactorily in the classroom. However, once some AS children are away from the school environment, their brains switch to 'refusal to do' mode. This is because children with AS tend to compartmentalise different areas of their lives. For example, learning and work happen at school and other things happen at home.

Strategies used by other parents of AS children include:

- Help with organisation – getting the right books and equipment ready, etc.

- Have a place and set time for homework and stick to it.

- Use incentives.

- With writing, which many AS children struggle with most, allow them to dictate while you type and then check together.

- Inform and negotiate with the school. As said, if your child presents few problems in class, the teacher(s) may be unaware. The amount and type of homework can be adjusted if they are made aware.

- Let your child make their own mistakes so they can learn from them.

- If your child is a perfectionist, teach them that everyone makes mistakes and that doing their best is the aim.

- Encourage your child to seek assistance from teachers.

- Break down what needs to be done into manageable steps.

- If possible, don't be the only one who deals with homework. Ask your partner to help with and supervise some of it.

- Keep calm.

Tips for teachers

The following tips may be useful for the teacher of the AS child:

- Remember that although the child's disability is invisible, it is no less real.

- ⬜ Every pupil with a diagnosis of AS is different. Please don't think that a particular child cannot possibly have AS because he/she is not like X who also has AS. Personality, IQ and difficulties will vary.

- Be patient when giving instructions and repeat them. Do not give too many instructions at once.

- Avoid using metaphorical language which a child with AS may well interpret literally.

- Children with AS find change difficult to cope with. Try to keep things the same as much as possible for the AS child, e.g. sitting in the same place, next to the same person, not changing coat peg order or book tray arrangements unnecessarily, etc.

- Point out any timetables or routine/rota lists you may have in the classroom and keep these in the same place.

- Children with AS often want friendships but find achieving and maintaining these difficult. Suggest ways the child could interact or join in with others if alone at breaktimes. Consult with the child and his/her parents over who the child likes or would like to be with/play with. Would arranged friendships/ buddy schemes work? Encourage the child to join clubs or groups at school where the activity is the main purpose and socialising is a secondary benefit.

- Some AS children have ritualistic behaviours which are very important and meaningful to them. Other children and teachers may not understand this and may think the child is just acting strangely or being odd. Remember and try to understand the significance of the child's ritualistic behaviours and encourage other pupils to be understanding too.

- For problems with social interaction, try the SOCCSS method:

- Situation – talk with the child about what happened, when, how and why.

- Options – let the child come up with possible things that can be done to resolve the situation.

- Consequences – look at each option together and decide good and bad points about them.

- Choices – let the child choose the best option.

- Strategy – make a plan together about how this will be done.

- Simulation – let the child practise carrying out their strategy with you or someone else.

(As described by Brenda Miles and Richard L Simpson in 'Effective Practices for Students with Asperger Syndrome, Focus on Exceptional Children', *Personal Communication*, J Roosa, 4 June 1997.)

An over-riding emotional state for those with ASDs is anxiety. Many undesirable behaviours will therefore stem from this anxiety which may be due to not understanding what to do, fear of doing something wrong, fear of being left out/ loneliness and fear of a change in routine. Some children with AS take medication for anxiety.

Whatever the reason for the onset of a tantrum, give the child with AS space to cool down – speak gently and reassuringly. Your usual firm and loud voice for controlling such behaviour may make things worse as a child with AS is usually oversensitive to sound and voice level. You may think you are just speaking firmly but the child may hear this as 'screaming'.

In dealing with tantrums, some teachers use a card signal system, e.g. holding up a certain card means, 'go to the quiet area to calm down'. This is because the child may be unable to take in verbal instructions in this state. Continue to supervise from a distance and once the episode is over you can talk and implement any needed consequences.

The child's parents may need extra updating and reassuring about their child's performance and progress in school, especially if the diagnosis is recent or there has been a change of class, increase or decrease of any medication, change of teacher or school, a change in the timetable or if there are impending examinations.

Remember, many children with AS have few behaviour problems in school that impact on others, but this does not mean they are not difficult at home. These children may well release all their frustrations, tiredness and anxiety at home, causing their parents enormous stress and strain.

Bullying

Because children with AS are often perceived as being different and have problems with communication and social skills, they can become targets for bullies. If your child is being bullied, find a way to get them to tell you what is happening and speak to your child's teacher.

The signs of bullying can be refusal or reluctance to go to school, being sad or depressed, physical injury, behaving violently at home, missing or damaged personal items, a lowering of self-esteem, fear of social situations and avoidance of certain places.

The National Autistic Society has a very helpful section on its website which offers ideas and support in dealing with bullying, including text and Internet bullying. The Society's helpline can also put you in touch with social skills training groups for ASD youngsters which might help your child. The Anti-Bullying Alliance charity has a lot of useful advice and links to resources too.

Behaviour problems

Because your child has AS, this doesn't mean that they will have behaviour problems. Some AS children appear to be models of good behaviour both at school and at home. Others can appear to be defiant, verbally and physically aggressive and, a lot of the time, very exhausting to parents.

You may have spent many years thinking and hoping that your child will grow out of this horror stage any time soon – but then find that it never happens. Why is this and what can you do to help your child and yourself?

What you perceive as difficult behaviour is largely the result of your child's intolerance to certain stimuli or situations, e.g. noise and other sensory sensitivities, frustration over changes in routine, having to cope with learning and social situations, and difficulty coping with the emotions and needs of others. All of the issues discussed in this chapter can cause your AS child anxiety which in turn can cause the resultant 'difficult' behaviour.

Coping strategies suggested by parents whose AS children range from six to 18 include the following:

- To help reduce the likelihood of your child refusing to go somewhere or to do something he/she needs to do, prepare for the event/situation well in advance. Talk through exactly what will happen, who will be there and what you will do. Use photographs, maps and diagrams. If your child knows what to expect in the new situation, this will help alleviate some of the fear or anxiety.

- Think ahead to some extent (but not obsessively). You may be able to help your child avoid some stressful situations.

- Don't protect your child from every anxiety provoking situation or he/she will never learn to deal with them or develop the confidence to do so.

- Develop some good strategies for dealing with tantrums (see earlier section).

- Develop and offer incentives for the desired behaviour and rewards for achieving it. This can work well even with older children. The idea is to create the will or drive to perform the desired behaviour.

- Be firm about what is unacceptable, e.g. verbal and physical abuse is not acceptable. Use loss of privileges rather than 'time out' to deal with this. Make sure you stick to it!

Some children with AS also have ADHD or ADD. Where that is the case, proper professional help and advice needs to be sought. If you have serious concerns about your child's behaviour, seek professional advice.

Be firm about what is unacceptable, e.g. verbal and physical abuse is not acceptable. Use loss of privileges rather than "time out" to deal with this and stick to it.

Summing Up

Many children with AS excel academically and are able to learn compensatory techniques that enable them to cope with the things at school that they find difficult. When parents and teachers are fully aware and understanding of an individual child's needs and how these change over time, the child has a greater chance of reaching their full potential at school.

6

Beyond School for the Young AS Person

Some young people with AS, just like some non-AS teenagers, appear to move seamlessly from school to college, university or work without too much difficulty. Others find this time of change and increasing independence very stressful and problematic.

As soon as the mountain climb of compulsory education is finally behind you, you and your child discover a new set of concerns waiting to be tackled.

Parents' concerns

It is generally agreed amongst the experts that the young person with AS is emotionally and socially behind his or her neuro-typical peers. (Expert and psychologist Tony Attwood believes by at least three years). You might, therefore, assume that when other older teenagers and young 20 somethings are experiencing independent living and serious relationships for the first time, some AS youngster won't be getting to that stage until their mid to late 20s at least. There may well be times when you wonder if they will ever reach that stage at all.

> You will want your child to be as independent as possible and to make their own decisions about their future.

If things begin to go wrong (perhaps your young adult has dropped out of college, is unable to work out what work he/she wants to do or is unable to get a job), an all pervading feeling of panic can creep over you. In one respect, any problems at this stage are no different to any problems from your child's past stages – meaning they will be resolved in your child's unique and possibly slower than average way. Of course, they are different in that you will want your child to be as independent as possible and to make their own decisions about their future.

There is no doubt that there will be times when you feel fearful for your child's future. If progress towards independence is slow then this can feel exasperating. Well-meaning friends may tell you that their child is just the same, yet often this only increases your sense of worry and concern. Unless that well-meaning friend's adolescent also has AS then the friend is not experiencing the same problems.

In these moments of panic, as parents of any child, I think we can only remind ourselves that we need to accept our nearly grown-up child the way he/she is. All we can do now is our best to support and encourage. When you do that you are no different to any other parent with any other child.

Problem areas

Problem areas for the young adult with AS can include:

- Choosing training, qualifications or a job.
- Managing in the world of work.
- Relationships.
- Anxieties and emotional needs.

Advice for young adults

When deciding what to do to resolve a particular problem or make a particular decision, you might find it useful to make a 'next step plan'. A 'next step plan' is a proposed, flexible course of action that takes needs, aspirations and circumstances into account as you move from one situation to the next.

If you are a young person with AS, you may like to devise a realistic plan for yourself and do this with a parent, friend or other person who knows you well.

If you are the parent of an older AS teenager, you might want to take the points of such a plan into account when advising and supporting your young person.

The 'next step plan' can be divided into three phases:

- Stage one: deciding what to do.
- Stage two: embarking on your plan.
- Stage three: keeping it going.

Training and work

Stage one: deciding what to do

Ask yourself	Possible answers	Points to consider
What do I like doing and what am I good at?	Working alone. DIY.	Non team work jobs. Jobs that involve practical skills.
What environments do I like?	Being outdoors.	Outdoor jobs.
What are my best subjects?	Maths and science.	Jobs that involve logical problem solving.
	There may be a job that involves your special interest area.	Make a list of what you are good at – ask others who know you well to help.
What don't I like doing and what am I not so good at?	Coping with lots of change. Dealing with people.	Consider jobs that tend to have a routine nature to them. Avoid jobs that are 'people orientated', e.g. social care.

What do I like doing and what am I good at?

Stage two: embarking on your plan

Ask yourself	Possible answers	Points to consider
Do I have enough skills or qualifications now? Can I use the skills and qualifications I have now?	No. Yes.	Find courses and training. Look for entry level jobs. Get careers advice. Visit recruitment centres. Consider contacting the National Autistic Society Prospects for possible further support (see chapter 7). It can take time – keep busy while you wait for your job or course to start.
What else do I need?	A CV (curriculum vitae). Interview techniques. Organisational skills.	Check out websites such as mymonster.co.uk for advice about content of CVs and interview techniques. Get smart or suitable clothing, plan your transport to get to and from your job, college or interview.
How will I manage? How can I get support at work or college?	By sorting out living arrangements in advance, if you are not going to be living at home. Have a mentor who can support and encourage you – a teacher, work colleague, friend, etc.	Know how much rent you can afford first, so that you know how much money you have left for other expenses. Give yourself time to get used to your new situation and routine. Always ask for advice or support if you need it.

Stage three: keeping it going

Ask yourself	Possible answers	Points to consider
How can I get on with others at work/college? What skills could I try to develop?	Listen carefully to instructions, ask for clarification if you need it and show interest in other people. Be reliable and conscientious.	Explain to the people closest to you at work or college what AS is and how it affects you. Be helpful to others and be flexible.
What do I do if I can't cope? What do I do if my job or course feels too difficult?	Decide exactly what it is that you can't cope with. Ask for advice or support. Leave.	Don't try to resolve problems on your own if they are too difficult. Be flexible – if you feel you are in the wrong job or doing the wrong thing then change to something else.

How can I get on with others?

Managing in the world of work

Stage one: deciding what to do

Ask yourself	Possible answers	Points to consider
How can I manage my money better?	Work out how much you need for essential expenses, e.g. rent and bills, and then you will know how much you have left for other things. Start a savings account. Check bank statements.	Avoid taking out loans and using credit cards. Ask family or friends who are good with money for advice.
How can I live independently? What if I want even more independence?	If you live at home, do your own washing and cleaning, and do the shopping or cooking sometimes. If it is financially feasible and you want to, look for your own flat/bedsit/ shared accommodation away from your parents.	Don't try to be independent with everything at once. If you find something difficult, e.g. cooking for yourself, keeping up with paying bills, etc then ask for advice. The more you do something, the better you will get at it.

Stage two: embarking on your plan

Ask yourself	Possible answers	Points to consider
Where do I want to live?	At home.	Pay your parents some rent.
Who do I want to live with?	With friends: look for shared accommodation together that you can all afford.	Do your share of the chores. Have a rota or agreement for chores, etc.
Where can I live if I find it stressful living with others all the time?	On my own: look for affordable accommodation.	Make sure you are within reachable distance of work or college. If you are renting, check the landlord's contracts carefully. Buy the essentials for your new home before luxuries. Have a house warming party – people might give you things you will need!
What if I'm not sure and might change my mind?	Find somewhere that has a shorter term contract – a few months or not more than a year.	Give yourself time to get used to your new living arrangements.

Stage three: keeping it going

Ask yourself	Possible answers	Points to consider
Where do I find people to deal with breakdowns, repairs, etc.	Landlord if renting. Look for registered trades people in the telephone directory or ask neighbours or others if they can recommend someone reliable.	You might want to take out insurance if you can afford it for gas, electricity, equipment, etc. This may give you access to emergency breakdown services.
What do I do about keeping up with bills?	Pay them straight away. Keep a record of what you pay.	You could consider paying by direct debit. Estimate about how much you need for bills each month and ensure you have that amount reserved for that purpose.
What about housework?	You will need to vacuum carpets or rugs, wash floor tiles, keep bathroom and kitchen areas hygienic, put rubbish out to be collected, etc.	Make sure your home is hygienic and safe. Observe the comments of others who visit you – or ask their opinion. Find special products for particular cleaning tasks such as non-smear glass cleaners and antibacterial cleaners for kitchens and bathrooms.

Relationships

Stage one: deciding what you want

Ask yourself	Possible answers	Points to consider
What kind of friends do I want?	People to share my interests with. A more intimate friend.	Join clubs or groups for people who share your interests.
How do I make friends? What can I do to meet people?	Join in more social events. Join clubs or groups for people who share your interests. Be interested in other people. Meet others who also have AS. Join Internet forums for people with similar interests.	Consider at what point you disclose your AS – it's your decision. Honesty may be best in the end. Listen to others – don't dominate the conversation. Be complimentary. Another person with AS will understand your difficulties with social communication.
How do people meet girlfriends/boyfriends?	They may start as friends first from college, work or other places. Social events. Dating/Internet dating agencies.	Don't go alone or be alone with someone you have only spoken to online before. Meet with others around until you know them properly.

Stage two: embarking on your plan

Ask yourself	Possible answer	Points to consider
How do I know if someone wants an intimate relationship or not?	They might say if you ask. Non-verbal clues: they will be physically affectionate, e.g. handholding, hugging, kissing, and will initiate this too.	Always respect the other person's decision if they do not want an intimate relationship with you. Your rule is: no means no.
How do I ask someone for a date?	You need to actually ask: face to face or by phone or email.	Keep the other person's interests in mind when deciding what to do or where to go – give them a choice of places and times.
What do I do if they say no?	You could ask again on another occasion (the time or day may have been inconvenient). If it's no again then assume they aren't interested.	Everyone risks being turned down. It's not you. It's not just about having shared interests. People are either attracted to each other or they are not. Keep meeting and getting to know other people.

Stage three: keeping a relationship going

Ask yourself	Possible answer	Points to consider
What keeps intimate relationships going?	Physical attraction, shared interests and the ability to emotionally support each other.	It can be difficult for people with AS to develop intimate relationships with NT people due to the differences in thinking, outlook and needs.
How do I keep a relationship going? What else helps?	It has to be a mutual decision. Make time for seeing each other and don't stop being interested in your partner – show interest in them as a person, not just in what they do or in what they do for you!	If the relationship is meant to be then it will feel right for both of you. Don't forget it's important to look nice. Being clean, wearing clean clothes and smelling nice is important too.

Being yourself

The most important thing to remember when making decisions about jobs, what course to do or what type of friends you would like is to be true to yourself. If you are a young person with AS, don't think that you have to live up to other people's expectations if those expectations do not take account of your personal abilities, aspirations or personality.

Whatever decisions you need to make, use the advice and information others can offer to make your own decision. Live by the three B rule! That's be yourself, believe in yourself and better yourself.

Anxieties and emotional needs

Everyone has everyday concerns and problems to sort out and most of these we take in our stride or may even expect. They are just the challenges of normal living.

Occasionally, situations arise that cause extra or long term anxiety and worry. As a young person with AS, you have the additional problem of not only facing an unfamiliar situation, but of coping with the higher than average anxiety level which is part of the condition.

'Live by the three B rule! That's be yourself, believe in yourself and better yourself.'

Advice for parents

If you're the parent of a young adult with AS, you might find your child reacts to additional stress either by becoming over emotional in terms of aggression or by appearing to do nothing to resolve the situation and sinking into apathy or depression. Your young AS adult may be unwilling to discuss how they are feeling, so it can feel difficult to know how to help. Perhaps the best method is to let them know you are available to:

- Support and advise.

- Make suggestions.

- Give examples of times in your own life when things have gone wrong and explain how the situation was resolved in the end.

- Point them in the right direction if you feel they need additional support or help.

Summing Up

Moving from the world of school to the world of work or college is not easy. It can pose a new set of challenges for both the young person and their parents.

With the right support and advice, most young people with AS will find they can eventually begin to be independent and embark on a career of their choice. When problems with living independently, work or relationships arise, much can be done to reduce anxiety by taking a logical and common sense step-by-step approach.

When helping your young adult to work through problems, always encourage them to decide what they want for themselves and to build on their many strengths and good points.

- If your young AS adult is still living at home, encourage them to be independent and do their share of the chores.

- Make use of careers guidance services either locally or online – see help list.

- Currently, the charity Contact A Family has information on options beyond 16 for young people with special needs.

- Check out the Asperger's Syndrome Foundation website for useful information about points to consider when finding work, training and dealing with relationships. Visit www. aspergerfoundation.org.uk.

The Adult with AS

f you are an adult with AS, it may be that over the years you have learnt to camouflage and compensate for any difficulties that you have. Perhaps a recent diagnosis of AS was the result of your own concerns or due to worries from others close to you.

Years ago, before AS was diagnosed in adults, those affected got on with their lives in much the same way as anyone else. Any difficulties individuals had with social interaction, sensory intolerances or relationships would have been put down to personality or temperament. It is therefore not surprising to find many older adults, unaware that they have the syndrome, leading apparently full and fulfilling lives – careers, interests, relationships and often marriage and children too.

Having AS does not mean that you cannot lead a good, happy and 'normal' life. But it does mean that you need to take your personal difficulties into account when making decisions about what is desirable and realistic for your own life.

Living alone may be ideal for one person with AS, but being married and having children may work equally well for another person. It is important to remember that having AS does not equal a particular life-style or set of problems; every person is different and their life will be as individual as they are. This is true whether you have AS or not.

> Every person who has AS is different and their life will be as individual as they are.

Adults with AS may experience problems in any of the following areas of life.

Employment

Getting a job

Currently, the National Autistic Society says that in the UK only 16% of adults who have ASDs and are of working age are in full time employment at any one time. Over three quarters of 2,000 people with autism surveyed said they would like to work. Four in ten have never worked. See autism facts and history at www.autism.org.uk.

Many adults with AS do have good and successful jobs and careers. Those I have met include computer programmers, lecturers, physicists, civil engineers and doctors. If you have the AS form of autism, you may be more likely, or even much more likely, to work or have a good career than those with the more severe form of autism. However, some adults with AS may have a learning disability that makes working difficult, and there are those with just AS who still experience employment problems.

Barriers to getting employment for some people with AS are often in connection with the wording of job vacancies which stress 'good communication skills' when this is not strictly necessary. Interviewees also normally need to show good interaction skills and, of course, finding this difficult is part of the condition.

It might also be difficult for you to keep a job because you feel anxious about work load, time keeping or doing well. However, the National Autistic Society offer different types of support from coaching, cv writing and supporting employment with social enterprises. Contact them to enquire or search their website Work section.

Disability employment advisors in JobCentre Plus offices can also inform and advise you. To make use of this service, you need to have had a formal diagnosis.

The Equality Act 2010 states that employers must make reasonable adjustments for the adult in the workplace. If you have a diagnosis of AS, it might be worth letting your employer or prospective employer know so that your needs can be taken into account.

The Equality Act 2010 states that employers must make reasonable adjustments for the adult in the workplace.

Keeping a job

If you have found an area of work you enjoy and are good at, the chances are that you will become a committed, reliable and loyal employee. Problems at this later stage can be related to working alongside others, getting support and coping with changes in routine.

You might like to consider the following strategies for keeping yourself going in your chosen career:

- Find a mentor at work or outside of work so that you have someone to talk to about your difficulties.

- Make a 'workplace map' that will remind you where particular rooms or people are if routines change or people move.

- Concentrate on the satisfaction you get from actually doing your job.

Advice to employers

- Employees with AS are generally loyal, committed, perfectionist and hardworking. The vast majority have average or well above average intelligence and many are extremely well qualified or capable of achieving high level qualifications.

- As well as the usual formal interview, give the prospective AS employee a trial work period that will better indicate his/her suitability to the job.

- Instructions need to be clear and to the point. Give the employee written versions of instructions, not just verbal.

- Give the employee plans or 'maps' of the office or working environment that show who and what is where.

- Unnecessary changes to routines or the immediate environment of the employee may cause stress and anxiety.

- They may have a commendable grasp of their subject or area of expertise, but need plenty of practice in training or supervising others. This is because they may find it hard to see where another person's difficulty with understanding lies.

Social life and friendships

If making friends or forming closer relationships is something you want but find hard to achieve, you could try the following strategies. All are suggestions from adults with AS.

- Join clubs or organisations where you can meet others with your interests.

- Accept invitations to social events if you can.

- Don't dominate conversations – ask the other person questions about what they do, what they like and what they think about things.

- Be well groomed.

- Practise conversational skills on online forums.

Marriage and intimacy

Many adults with AS decide that the stress of living intimately with someone is not for them. Others, however, do choose long term intimate relationships and/or marriage and children. This can give rise to problems related to living alongside and accommodating the needs of others.

What may be difficult?

Research has shown that people with AS can take longer to develop the skills of empathy and reciprocity far enough to enable such relationships to work. It might be that your partner is telling you that there are problems in the relationship but you are having difficulty in understanding what these are. Your partner may be saying things like:

- 'You don't give me emotional support'.
- 'You don't initiate doing things in the home or with the children'.
- 'You criticise the children too much'.
- 'You don't seem interested in me as a person'.

These statements may be confusing and no matter how hard you try to follow instructions, you may find you are still not getting it right.

If this is the case then it would be a good idea to seek professional advice, i.e. counselling via a therapist trained in working with AS relationships. You should attend this couple's counselling together as this will enable you both to develop a deeper understanding of your different ways of thinking and seeing things. You both need to understand the limitations that one of you having AS imposes on an intimate relationship. At the same time, you both also need to know how to amplify the many good points your relationship has.

You and your partner may also find it helpful to get to know other couples with the same AS/NT relationship. There may be local groups of the National Autistic Society in your area or other organisations for those with AS.

Reading some of the many anecdotal books written by those on the spectrum and their partners can also offer useful insight and guidance for both of you. *Asperger Syndrome – A Love Story* by Sarah Hendrickx and Keith Newton, *An Asperger Marriage* by Gisela and Christopher Slater-Walker and *Alone Together* by Katrin Bentley are just a few examples.

Counsellor and Asperger expert Maxine Aston has also written books about coping in AS/NT relationships. This includes *The Asperger Couple's Workbook* (see book list). Remember, though, all relationships and all couples are different.

See chapter 9 for more information on the benefits of couple's counselling.

Parenting

Parenting can pose particular problems if you are an adult with AS. Children and adolescents can be exhausting, irrational, demanding and erratic – they are designed to try the patience of their parents whether AS is involved or not! Of course they are also a great joy and privilege – the human race would not have got very far without them. Chapter 10 deals with parenting issues in more detail.

When you need support

Welfare and benefits

The maze of the tax and benefits system in the UK can be confusing. Any benefits you may be entitled to will be either non means-tested or means-tested.

For up-to-date information on benefits and advice about how to claim, visit the Citizens Advice Bureau website or the National Autistic Society website, where you will find a section on benefits. See help list for contact details.

Emotional support

If you think you are experiencing extra stress or anxiety, or that you may be depressed, there are plenty of people and support organisations whose job it is to help you.

If you think you are experiencing extra stress or anxiety, or that you may be depressed, there are plenty of people and support organisations whose job it is to help you.

You may find you can contact one of the groups that there are for adults with AS. Some of these are local groups or online forums where you can meet and talk. The advantage of these groups is that you meet other adults who understand AS, problems that may be related to having AS and your approach to dealing with problems.

A few specialist counselling services also exist for adults with AS. Contact the National Autistic Society's helpline and ask if there is a group near you or within a reachable distance (www.autism.org.uk). Alternatively, various mental health charities or organisations may have support groups and counselling services in your area, e.g. MIND (the National Association for Mental Health).

Research shows that large numbers of adults with AS suffer from anxiety related disorders or depression at some point in their lives. This may be due to trying to cope with social interaction and relationships, managing living independently, loneliness and financial difficulties.

Having AS, a communication disorder, means that you may not be able to convey your concerns and feelings and so get the advice and support you need from family or friends. You may keep quiet about problems. Many adults with AS suppress their emotions and tell themselves that this is just the way life is. It may not occur to you that others can make helpful and practical suggestions, so it is a good idea to investigate what support there is. If you are depressed it is also important to get professional medical advice rather than ignoring your symptoms.

Dealing with bullying

Many adults with AS experience some form of bullying in the workplace or elsewhere. While some feel able to ignore and deal with this, others are badly affected.

- Remember it is not your fault and you have done nothing wrong.
- Find someone to talk to. If you are distressed then counselling or having a 'mentor' can be very beneficial.
- Look into ways of being more assertive and responding in ways the bully would not expect.
- Try to understand the bully's motives – this will help you feel less fearful. Most adult bullies lead sad, unhappy lives.
- Find out about your employer's policy on bullying.
- Tell your employer what is happening if you can.
- Contact support and advice agencies such as SupportLine or Trades Union Congress (TUC) (see help list).

OCD

OCD is not the same as autistic ritualistic behaviour, preference for routine or inflexibility in ways of doing things. OCD is about having intrusive thoughts known as obsessions.

Someone with OCD performs compulsive actions or rituals to alleviate the anxiety caused by the obsession. This makes the obsession or fear feel safe or subside momentarily and so reduces the anxiety. Compulsions include constant checking, hoarding, ruminating, touching and hair pulling. The underlying fears or obsessions can include fear of contamination, fear of harm coming to yourself or others, hypochondria and fear of not being perfect.

There is a lot of research that is investigating the connection between biomedical, nutritional and environmental factors and ASDs.

OCD can develop to such an extent that sufferers are unable to perform everyday tasks or take part in everyday activities due to their fears. They live in a constant state of alertness and anxiety, becoming isolated and housebound. That may sound extreme, but OCD is actually the second most common mental illness after depression.

If you think you have OCD then it is important to get professional medical advice and treatment. Start by going to your GP, who may refer you to a therapist. You may, under medical supervision, be offered medication to reduce anxiety, but you can also seek private treatment for yourself if you prefer.

OCD Action is a UK based charity which provides a good source of advice and information on this subject. They are a good starting point for finding out if you have OCD (they have an online questionnaire which can suggest whether or not such a diagnosis is likely), looking for places where you can get treatment throughout the UK and finding support groups.

Another UK based organisations is OCD UK. This provides information about treatment and support for sufferers and their families, including an advice line. IOCD UK has an online support forum for sufferers (see www.ocdforums.org).

Immunity and nutrition

There are many theories that suggest our moods, behaviours and emotions are influenced by our environment or diet. There is some research that is investigating the connection between biomedical, nutritional and environmental factors and ASDs.

Some theories claim significant benefits to those who follow particular regimes of lifestyle or diet. Many experts believe these claims are still in the early stages of research and are unproven. If you want to look further at these biomedical, autoimmune or dietary interventions, there are many websites that outline the theories. See Autism Research Institute in the help list.

Relaxation

Suggested techniques for relaxing and de-stressing:

- Having time on your own away from other people every day.
- Having an absorbing hobby or interest that you can do on your own, e.g. computer games or crosswords.
- Having an absorbing hobby or interest that you can do with like-minded people, e.g. chess.
- Having a mentor – someone who understands AS and who knows you, who can listen, advise and support.

Supported living

Some adults are unable to manage independent living and full-time employment, the problems of AS and/or having co-morbid conditions making this unrealistic and unmanageable. If this is you or an adult with AS you know, you might want to investigate one of the specialist community support environments.

Some specialist schools and colleges also have residential places for young people in their 20s and these can offer a gradual and manageable transition to more independent living.

If you are a member of the National Autistic Society, you will probably receive their quarterly magazine *Communication* which often contains information and points of contact for getting further information about these colleges and living environments. You will need to check out the individual settings yourself to see what suits and what is appropriate and helpful to your situation.

The benefits of living, working or training in a specialist supportive environment include:

- Access to helpful interventions.
- Suitable training or work.

- Teachers, carers and supervisors that are knowledgeable in AS.
- Support and advice available.
- A gradual and more manageable transition to a realistic amount of independence.
- The opportunity to move away from home and develop your own life.

Summing Up

Whether they have AS or not, everyone experiences difficulties and challenges at some point in different areas of their lives. No one is immune to this and there are plenty of self-help strategies, advice organisations and support services that we can use.

Adults with AS may occasionally experience particular difficulties and stresses. This may be due to finding communication or understanding others hard, or because they are suffering from some of the associated anxiety disorders that someone on the autistic spectrum may be prone to. It is often a question of acknowledging that you have a problem and then finding a solution or the support that helps you most.

8

Living with an AS Partner

t isn't easy living in a long term relationship with a partner who has AS. You will know this if you are someone who has been married or living with an AS partner for some years. If you are contemplating a serious relationship with someone who has AS then you would be well advised to think very carefully about the issues involved in such a partnership.

How do NT/AS relationships start?

The same as any other. You meet, you spend time with each other, you get on and you fall in love. No different to any other relationship. Many NT partners report having noticed odd or puzzling behaviours. If they didn't know that the person had AS, they might have put this down to personality, upbringing or misunderstandings.

Adults with AS who marry or embark on long term intimate relationships are those at the highest end of the spectrum. They are very often highly intelligent and qualified individuals with professional careers who, on the outside, appear to be living very successful and independent lives.

It isn't easy living in a long term relationship with a partner who has Asperger's syndrome.

If a person with AS develops a relationship then this is because they want that relationship. While some may want someone with whom to share thoughts and feelings, others may place less or very little importance on this normal aspect of an intimate relationship.

With the growth of dating agencies and access to online friendship forums, it has become much easier for those who have difficulties with social communication to meet potential partners. This is not a bad thing. The problem, however, may be that if an adult is unaware that they have AS (and a great many are unaware due to the fact that AS has only really been diagnosed in adults since the 1990s), relationships may be well established before problems begin.

Relationships with AS partners

If you are an NT partner with an AS partner, your reasons for starting a relationship may have included the following:

- You found your partner unusually and refreshingly honest, loyal and committed.

- You overlooked any unusual behaviours your partner may have had and put them down to rational explanations.

- You have had relationships with others showing similar characteristics in the past.

- You shared the same morals, ethics and level of intelligence.

- You believed you wanted the same things in life.

- You had shared interests.

- Your life had included having to care for or support others close to you.

- Your life had included not having your emotional needs met.

- You have had very few or no other intimate relationships in the past and so had nothing to compare.

- None of your friends or family noticed your partner's AS and so you were not alerted to any possible problems.

It is easy to see, then, how the AS can have been overlooked. I also think it is true to say that AS is very often not seen as a problem by the person who actually has it. Your partner may have thought every one else was like them. The AS traits are therefore likely to place burdens and stress on those who live with the adult AS person rather than the sufferer themselves. What often happens is that the NT partner, unaware of the undiagnosed disorder, blames other things for the difficulties.

AS is an invisible disorder, so it can be very difficult to talk to friends and family about the problems associated with it. Your AS partner will also have learnt techniques for coping and behaving in different social situations. Unfortunately, as a result, this can mean that your problems are not believed by other people.

When AS is discovered

If you didn't know your partner had AS when you met, the discovery may have been made after a number of difficulties arose. For some couples, the discovery is made when one of their children is diagnosed with AS. For others, they recognise their own situation when they hear or read of others with the same kind of relationship. AS can also come to light when the person who has it is being treated for another condition like anxiety or depression.

Effects on the NT partner

The effects can be placed in three groups. Firstly are the effects that are due to the AS partner's difficulty or inability to read the emotions of their partner or to show interest in their partner as a person. Secondly are the effects of being self-absorbed and naturally interested only in what is happening in their own head. Thirdly are the effects of a general inability or unwillingness to understand their full role in the family.

Over time, you, the NT partner, may experience many of the following problems:

- Feeling ignored or not needed – your AS partner may have a greater than usual need for solitude and solitary pursuits.

- Feeling only wanted for what you do for your partner.

- Being deprived of emotional support – even when you are ill or bereaved. This is partly due to your partner being unable to imagine your needs.

- Lack of normal conversation due to your partner's inappropriate, pedantic or blunt responses. You can feel very put down.

- Your partner may have difficulty with initiating everyday chores within the home or for the family.

- If you have a child, you may feel that the overall burden and responsibility for parenting falls on you. Your partner may feel more like an extra child than an equal in the parenting stakes.

- You may have many misunderstandings that result in arguments or rows, perhaps due to your partner's literal interpretation of language or his/her high anxiety levels.

- Your life together may become dominated by your partner's dislike of change and need for routine.

- You may begin to give up things you once enjoyed or ambitions you once had. This could be the result of your partner's unintentional behaviour that causes your self-esteem, self-belief and confidence to erode.

- You may lose spontaneity and the ability to simply be yourself because you begin to think twice about how your partner will react i.e. with disinterest, disapproval, criticism, etc. What is the point in being yourself when it is not appreciated?

Your life together may become dominated by your partner's dislike of change and need for routine.

- You may become isolated because your friends may not understand your situation or do not get on with your partner.

- You may suffer panic attacks, anxiety disorders or depression. A form of emotional deprivation disorder has been identified as a condition NT partners can suffer from. Different terms are used to describe this by different mental health professionals and include emotional abuse, affective deprivation disorder or CAD - see the 'Taking care of yourself' section later in the chapter.

- You may lose all faith in your relationship – about 80% of marriages where one partner has AS result in divorce.

- You may be baffled as to why your partner can be so brilliant in some respects (and many adults with AS are physicians, scientists, engineers, etc) but so immature and disabled when it comes to social and emotional matters.

Reactions to the diagnosis

When you discover that the difficulties in your relationship are due to your partner having AS, this may come as a relief. It can help both of you to know that the problems are no one's fault and are not deliberate.

Your reactions may include the following:

- Disbelief that you didn't know.

- Feeling a sense of loss for the person you thought you had married/committed to.

- Anger.

- Depression.

- Wanting to leave the relationship.

- Choosing to stay. This can take a lot of courage. If it sounds too difficult then make it 'choosing to stay for now'. It can be difficult believing that you will find a way to manage all the problems, but if your reason for choosing to stay is that you still love your partner and are convinced he/she still loves you, you both have a firm foundation for finding a way to live with AS.

If your reason for choosing to stay is that you still love your partner and are convinced he/she still loves you then you both have a firm foundation for finding a way to live with AS.

Strategies for coping

Take time

How you feel in the aftermath of your partner's diagnosis may not be how you'll feel for ever – so give yourself time.

Get the facts straight

Find out everything you can about AS. Read, research and talk to others in similar situations. The more you understand the disorder, the more help you can get for yourself and your partner.

Never discount the good

If you have been together a long time, there are bound to be aspects of your relationship and your life together that are very good. It can be helpful to think back to the early days of being in love and remembering what brought you together in the first place. Those reasons may still be there and will be important to you. If you have had children together, you will have a special bond in that respect too.

Communication – a new way

To your AS partner, the prime purpose of communication is to give or receive information. A person with AS is generally not interested in someone else's thoughts or feelings unless they have a personal need for that information. You, though, will often need to communicate with others because you need to connect, share and receive support. You probably find that it is difficult or impossible to have a normal chatty conversation with your AS partner.

Sometimes it can seem that someone with AS is refusing to answer a question that you've asked. However, this can just be because the person with AS needs a few seconds to process the question and answer. In this time you might actually offer yourself a response. This, of course, is no good; you need to wait for the response.

Another difficulty is with misunderstanding. Your AS partner may become quite irate if you exaggerate a situation. For example, a sentence like 'I waited hours at the post office! If I hadn't got to the front of the queue when I did, I would have died!' would sound confusing and stupid to someone with AS. If your partner is someone who finds exaggeration difficult and annoying then avoid using it.

Another point to remember is to talk about one subject or issue at a time. The thought hopping that non-AS people are able to do can be extremely stressful and impossible to keep up with.

A place to talk

Find the right time and place to have a discussion. Expecting your partner to engage in a conversation about why you're thinking of giving your job up while you're both washing up with the radio on and the dog barking in the background, might be too much to ask. For these and other deep conversations, try the three no's rule:

- No other people to interrupt.
- No distractions.
- No time constraints.

You may then find that your AS partner is able to offer logical and rational advice.

Be specific

If you want or need a particular response and know your partner is unlikely to be able to give this, tell them exactly what it is you need from the conversation. For example, if you just say that you have had a bad day at work, you might get no response. However, instead you could tell you partner that, e.g., it would help if they gave you a hug or cooked the dinner.

Say what you need and give your partner a chance to help.

Using 'I'

Always using the word 'I' or 'me' is another useful tip. Don't say: 'When you do that it's really irritating'. Say: 'I feel irritated when you do that'.

Don't say: 'No one likes being ignored. It would make anyone upset'. You really mean: 'I feel upset because you are ignoring me right now'.

People with AS need direct, explicit language. If they are to understand us then we need to get into the habit of talking to them that way.

Encouraging your partner's support

People with AS sometimes give little thought to initiating things outside of normal routines. They can be quite happy wrapped up with their own thoughts and (quite often) solitary activities. This can make life as a couple and family difficult. If you want your partner to be the one to sort something out, just ask. Don't moan that your partner never helps – say what you need as well and give your partner the chance to help.

A word of caution – having asked your partner to make the decision and do the choosing, make sure you go with whatever he/she comes up with. If you don't, why would they want to bother responding to your request again? If you think there is a very real risk of something totally inappropriate being chosen, have a list of suggestions and ask your partner to pick and organise one. This helps to remove the burden of feeling that you are always the one to make choices, initiate changes, sort out events, etc. It helps create a better balanced relationship and family life.

Outbursts and tantrums

Simply not being understood can cause great frustration for someone with AS. Your partner may struggle to explain their reasoning behind something and become totally exasperated if you don't understand. If your partner's effort to do something or get somewhere is thwarted by others, this can also be another trigger for a flare up.

So what can you do? My general rule for myself is to keep out of it as far as possible and encourage anyone else around to do the same. If you can see the solution and feel you need to intervene then wait for a space in the ranting and put your suggestion simply and clearly. Don't argue or tell him/her that they are making a fuss about nothing. This is fruitless and will only flame the flare up further.

Once it's all over it can be remarkable how quickly normal temperaments are resumed.

Verbal and physical abuse

This should not be tolerated by anyone in any relationship. If this is an issue for you then you should both seek professional advice and help.

Simply not being understood can cause great frustration for someone with AS.

Bananas!

This stands for 'blame all nuttiness and niggliness on AS'. You take a piece of paper and draw a line down the middle. At the top of one column you write 'AS' and at the top of the other column you write 'the real person'. Under AS you list all those undesirable behaviours and characteristics that are caused by the condition. Under the real person you list all those endearing and amazing characteristics and talents your partner possesses.

Your table might look a bit like this:

AS	The real person
Communication problems.	Honest, loyal, sense of humour.
Obsessive ways of doing things.	Moral standards.
Difficulty with spontaneity and initiative.	Hard working.
Little reciprocity.	Gentle.
	Loyal.
	Sense of humour.
	Commitment to family.

Continue adding to the lists until you have at least five more good personal characteristics than AS ones. Of course, there are many not so good personal characteristics (and everyone has a mixture of good and bad characteristics), but there are also many good characteristics associated with having AS. However, the purpose of the 'bananas' technique is to give you a way to place the blame for the problems. It is a way of externalising anger or hurt. If the neurological differences in the brain make-up of people with AS cause the differences and difficulties, why not blame the condition rather than the person?

When it is hard to cope with someone's behaviour or responses, this is a way of separating the person from the condition. The AS can almost become a third party in your relationship and you can blame it (not your partner) for quite a lot! This does mean, of course, that you need to be aware of what problems are due to AS and what are down to personality or selfish behaviour. AS can only take the blame for the behaviours/difficulties it causes.

Shared interests

> Finding something you can do together can enhance your sense of being a couple – a couple engaged in shared time and enjoyment.

Some couples find that, as time goes by, they don't have many shared interests other than the upbringing of their children. If your relationship has become that way, try to enjoy more time or specific activities together again. It doesn't have to be anything spectacular, but finding something you can do together can enhance your sense of being a couple – a couple engaged in shared time and enjoyment.

Physical intimacy

For many couples, this side of the relationship has never been a problem.

However, the physical side of the relationship can be a problem for some couples. The reasons can include: the AS partner losing all interest in sex once he/she has tried it, the AS partner finding touch and holding uncomfortable due to sensory over-sensitivities, the NT partner disliking a missing emotional element or depression and anxiety on the part of one partner.

As the key to resolving such issues is communicating with each other, this can pose problems. But help is at hand. There are a great number of self-help books that offer suggestions – particularly books written for those in AS relationships (see the book list for ideas). You may even find one to read together. More importantly, you could also find someone to talk to – a close friend or relative, someone else in an AS relationship or through counselling or couple's counselling (again, it is important to find a counsellor experienced in helping those with AS).

The important thing is that if you are unhappy with the physical side of your relationship and want it to change, you must take steps to resolve this. Leaving it will only result in growing resentment.

If the problems cannot be resolved, this will become another factor to consider as you decide whether the relationship as a whole is working.

Project you

Your relationship with your AS partner might be a very big part of your life, but it's not everything. It can be a good idea to develop your life in other areas too – friendships, jobs, careers, absorbing interests, beliefs. Doing this can help combat the feelings of loneliness, depression and low self-esteem that can set in after many years of living in an AS relationship.

If it's your choice to stay in the relationship, it's up to you to find the things that help fill the gap created by the lack of real emotional support or connection.

Taking care of yourself

Maxine Aston, counsellor and AS expert (www.maxineaston.co.uk), describes the following as signs of emotional deprivation:

- Anxiety and panic attacks.
- Loss of confidence and self-esteem.
- Depression.
- Isolation and loneliness.

If you believe the difficulties in your relationship are causing you to suffer in the above ways, you need to take steps to help yourself. Sadly, the AS partner is very often unaware that the relationship is having this effect on their NT partner. If they are made aware, they are usually still unable to provide the emotional support you need.

Maxine Aston describes this emotional deprivation as 'Cassandra affective disorder' or CAD (www.maxineaston.co.uk, see help list). Cassandra was a mythical character who was bestowed with great insight into other people but was under a curse of never being believed. She therefore became isolated and depressed, her distress reflecting the emotions felt by NT partners when their problems are not heard or understood by their AS partner or others.

However, there is good news. Much can be done to reduce and avoid these negative effects.

If you think your mental health is suffering because of your relationship, talk to your GP. They might suggest medication for depression or/and counselling. Counselling will give you someone to explore things with so you can make sense of why you are feeling the way you do (see chapter 9 for more information on counselling).

Other sources of advice and support include:

- Local support groups.

- Online web forums for those affected by AS.

- Supportive workshops for people with AS partners (see help list).

Working

Working in a job you enjoy can go a long way to promoting a sense of wellbeing and happiness. The more involved and happy you are in things outside of your relationship, the less focussed you will be on any problems that exist there. If you can find ways to be absorbed in things with people who respond to you in the more normal way, you will begin to feel more confident.

A sense of self and okay-ness

Whether we feel content or at peace with our lot in life is not entirely dependent on what we have or don't have, or even on how others treat us. It is about believing and feeling that the real you inside is okay.

Different people find different ways of achieving a sense of okay-ness. Some have a religious faith. Others practise meditation or yoga and find this gives them a way to nurture and strengthen themselves. Finding your own way to just 'be' can help you replenish your strength.

Psychologists talk about the importance of knowing ourselves and being in touch with our own needs. If we can do that we might find we can accept ourselves and others and see life in a different light. However, it can be difficult when you feel depressed and emotionally neglected to have the will to take action. Start by asking yourself: 'If I had a best friend who was suffering in this way, what would I advise and do for her/him?'

If you can find a way to live that is nurturing to you, you may discover that you can accept the things you cannot change, enjoy what is good in your life and your relationship, and develop the confidence to protect yourself from what harms you emotionally.

Friendships and family

If you are lucky enough to have family or close friends nearby, they can be a good source of comfort and support. If you don't have this then you need to prevent yourself from becoming isolated. A new job or developing new interests might be a way to do this – or getting back in touch with old friends. You may feel it is difficult to make new close friends due to the lack of understanding of AS and the effect it has on your relationship – but you might find that friends understand better than you think.

Work out a simple but accurate way of describing your partner's difficulties. Whether you decide to tell people about this is up to you, but I think it's generally true that really close and supportive friendships develop when people are most open and real about themselves.

Why bother?

If it sounds hard work finding the way to nurture and develop your relationship, you might find yourself asking if it is really worth it. Some couples decide it is not and that they are too different to continue the relationship.

It is very rare for the person with AS to initiate the ending of a relationship, but it can also be a very difficult decision for their partner to make. If you decide to stay you will know that although your AS partner cannot meet your emotional needs in the usual reciprocal way, you may have a different and equally valid connection that is also based on love, commitment, shared intimacy and simply going through life together.

> It can be difficult when you feel depressed and emotionally neglected to have the will to take action. Start by asking yourself: "If I had a best friend who was suffering in this way, what would I advise and do for her/him?"

So why stay?

- Because you have a strong bond and love each other.

- Because your relationship is based on love and promises to each other and you feel it's worth persevering.

- Because, in spite of the difficulties, you feel you have something good.

- Because life is about so much more than just getting what you need for yourself the easiest way you can.

- Because you choose to.

Summing Up

If you decide to stay in an intimate relationship with your AS partner, make sure you are staying for the right reasons. Your mental health and wellbeing (and that of your children if you have any) is more important than any sense of duty or belief that you must stay.

Your AS partner can only make a limited amount of change and it is true that you will be the one making most of the effort in making any changes. However, if you know that your relationship is still based on love and that your new knowledge and understanding of AS is enabling you both to live in a more fulfilling way with each other, you may decide that life with an AS partner can be the right one.

All relationships are different. Whether they last depends on the personalities, temperaments, past issues and experiences of both parties, not solely on whether one has AS or not. Some experts might give us the impression that someone with AS cannot be a soul mate because they cannot connect on an emotional level. Without that connection and reciprocity expected in an intimate relationship, how can they become a soul mate? However, those of us who live with an AS partner on a long term and intimate basis can also claim to be experts.

Only you will know whether or not there are moments when you do connect on a deeper level and whether that is enough for you. You will know your partner as an individual person not defined by AS.

9

Counselling Those Affected

Many people affected by AS decide to have professional counselling. Choosing to do this is not a sign of failure, but a positive step in finding ways to deal with various problems. Living with AS, whether you or someone close to you has it, can be exhausting and stressful, and not asking for help or the support you deserve does no one any good.

It is essential to choose a counsellor who knows what AS is and, preferably, is used to dealing with people who are affected by it. That may sound obvious, but research shows that while many people seek professional guidance in dealing with AS, the majority find it unhelpful or even that it makes their situation worse when they choose a therapist who is unfamiliar with AS and AS relationships. You can find an experienced person either by checking the information under a therapist's registration details or by contacting the National Autistic Society who have a short list of suitable counsellors.

> It is essential to choose a counsellor who knows what AS is and, preferably, is used to dealing with people who are affected by it.

As mentioned in previous chapters, qualified counsellors will be registered by the official counselling registration bodies. This means that they are sufficiently trained, qualified and experienced. These registering organisations include:

- British Association for Counselling and Psychotherapy (BACP).
- British Association for Sexual and Relationship Therapy (BASRT).
- British Psychoanalytic Council (BPC).
- Confederation of Scottish Counselling Agencies (COSCA).
- UK Association for Humanistic Psychology Practitioners (UKAHPP).
- United Kingdom Council for Psychotherapy (UKCP).

Finding a counsellor

You can find a counsellor by:

- Contacting your GP.
- Contacting one of the registering organisations just mentioned – they have lists of counsellors/therapists in different areas.
- Looking in your phonebook for local private practitioners.
- Contacting MIND (National Association for Mental Health) – see www.mind.org.uk.

- Contacting the National Autistic Society at autismhelpline@nas.org.uk. They can help you find a suitable counsellor whether you have an ASD yourself or are a relative or carer of someone who does. They can also give advice about affording the counselling bill.

Types of therapy

There are different types of therapy – some counsellors or therapists use more than one type.

Cognitive behavioural therapies

This includes cognitive behaviour therapy (CBT), rational emotive behaviour therapy, solution focussed therapy and acceptance and commitment therapy.

CBT is about helping people to understand how their thoughts and behaviour impact upon their emotions. Clients are taught how to recognise irrational/faulty thoughts and replace them with more accurate/pragmatic thoughts which help to bring about a change in perception, behaviour and emotion. CBT is recommended by NICE (the National Institute for Clinical Excellence) for the treatment of anxiety disorders and depression.

The National Autistic Society says that evidence suggests that CBT is often very helpful for people with ASDs. Search counselling at www.autism.org.uk.

The National Autistic Society says that evidence suggests that CBT is often very helpful for people with ASDs.

Psychodynamic

Psychodynamic therapy has also been found to be beneficial to those affected by AS. In psychodynamic therapy the client learns how their past experiences influence their present thinking and situation. This therapy lasts longer than CBT.

Humanistic

Again, this therapy is more long term compared to CBT. The aim of the humanistic therapist is to believe in the client's capabilities and to allow them to move at their own pace.

Types of humanistic therapy are:

- Person centred – the person's self concept is explored. The therapist listens empathetically and non-judgmentally, allowing the client to correct and develop their self-image.

- Gestalt – this is about promoting self awareness and the ability to support your own emotional needs.

- Transactional analysis – this is related to a theory that we have three 'ego states' ('parent', 'adult' and 'child') and that the way we are is the result of how we were treated and developed emotionally as children.

- Transpersonal psychology and psycho synthesis – here the client looks at their own personal view and is encouraged to discover deeper, spiritual aspects to themselves and so build on their qualities.

Counselling for a child with AS

Counsellors who are used to working with children who have ASDs will use methods that will help the child communicate in a less direct way.

There might be times when some form of counselling would help a child with AS. This might be in order to deal with a co-morbid condition, such as OCD, or to help the child deal with problems caused by the symptoms of their AS – social or school phobia, difficult behaviour, bullying, becoming aware that they are 'different', etc.

If you or a professional dealing with your child's problems decide that counselling might help, you will first need to convince your child of this and find a method that suits.

CBT may help a child overcome OCD. For other problems, a child with AS is very unlikely to be able to talk about their thoughts and feelings in the way a child without AS might be able to do. Forcing your child to go along to such sessions when they don't want to is likely to cause more anxiety, making therapy less successful.

Counsellors who are used to working with children who have ASDs will use methods that will help the child communicate in a less direct way (which is also less threatening for the child). Such methods may involve using visual materials such as charts and diagrams, or the CAT Kit which AS expert Tony Attwood helped devise (www.catkit-us.com).

CAT stands for cognitive affective training. It is a visual interactive communication game that allows therapists to become aware of the client's thoughts, emotions and feelings. At the same time, the child gains an insight into themselves and their behaviour.

Other methods include using Social Stories TM and different therapy methods that promote self knowledge and awareness, such as music therapy, dance and drama therapy or art therapy. With children who respond to them, these therapies can be a good way to develop social and communication skills.

The National Autistic Society's publication *Approaches to Autism* (NAS revised 2007) describes various types of therapies and interventions that can be tried (see book list).

Counselling for an adult with AS

Adults with AS may decide to seek counselling for themselves for various reasons.

These might include:

- Wanting help with developing social skills.
- Wanting help to find closer relationships.
- Wanting help to deal with depression or anxiety.
- Wanting to overcome OCD.
- Needing emotional support to deal with specific personal issues.

If you are an adult with AS, you might think you are unlikely to find talking about difficulties helpful. You may feel very uncomfortable discussing what you consider to be personal information. However, if you decide to give it a go then you might find that you can gain some useful strategies and ideas that actually do help. A counsellor who understands AS and those who have it will use methods that will suit your way of thinking.

Relationship counselling for the NT/AS couple

According to one statistics, about 75% of NT/AS couples seek counselling at some stage (Aspergers in Love: Couple Relationships and Family Affairs, Maxine Aston, Jessica Kingsley Publishers, 2008). This will probably have been initiated by the NT partner who may have begun to feel that they need advice and support.

Some couples do not realise that one of them definitely has AS at this stage. One of them may suspect it and an experienced and knowledgeable counsellor may confirm that this is probable. You might then both decide to get a firm diagnosis or assessment with someone qualified to do this.

Assuming you already know one of you has AS, the sessions you attend will take careful consideration of the AS partner's communication disabilities, i.e. the fact that your partner is very likely to have poor self-knowledge and problems with insight and empathy regarding you and your relationship together. Your AS partner is quite likely to hold a very different view of how your marriage or relationship is working and may have no understanding into what is really happening.

Remember that if you have to persuade your partner to attend then he/she will probably be feeling totally out of their comfort zone. Not only will they be unwilling to express thoughts and feelings, they may not actually know how to do this. However, you will find that some counsellors use charts and diagrams to record your information. This is because your AS partner will find it easier to make sense of a visual representation of your relationship than to merely sit and listen to you and the therapist talking about it.

Be aware that during counselling sessions with your AS partner, you may have to listen to him/her coming out with some pretty blunt stuff which you might not have heard before. Any misconceptions that you had about the relationship will certainly be put right, and it may be shocking to hear these views.

Going to counselling with your partner can help you and your relationship in several ways:

- It will give you the chance to talk about things that you might normally find difficult to talk about.

- It will help your partner accept that his/her condition really does have an effect on your relationship.

- It will enable him/her to hear your side of things from a third party.

- It will enable you to hear his/her side of things from a third party.

- It will enable you both to gain deeper insights into AS and relationships.

- It can help you parent more effectively together.

- It will help you map out a step-by-step way forward.

- It will help you to feel supported.

> Some couples do not realise that one of them definitely has AS at this stage. One of them may suspect it and an experienced and knowledgeable counsellor may confirm that this is probable.

Counselling for the parent or the NT partner

You might like to consider having counselling for yourself, even if you are also attending counselling with your AS partner. You will then have the opportunity to talk more openly about issues that you can't discuss in front of your partner.

As it is very likely that you will be the one making most of the effort to change and keep the relationship going in the way you need it to be, it is also likely that you will need someone with whom you can discuss how your strategies are going and how you are coping.

The same applies if you are a parent of a child with AS. Even if you have close friends and family, the objective and professional expertise of someone trained to help you work through problems and who can provide support and empathy can be enormously helpful.

Some people find support groups for parents or partners useful. If there isn't one in your area, could you start one? If you attend any of the National Autistic Society regional seminars or workshops, or if you have a child who has AS and attends an AS youth group, these would be good places to start to get to know others in the same situation.

If you are a partner seeking support, you could also attend some of the workshops that are run specifically for partners (see previous chapter and help list for further information). These and other support groups enable you to meet others in the same situation. You will be able to talk about the issues that effect you with those who know exactly what you are talking about. Although you would need to pay the fee to attend, some social services are willing to help attendees with the cost as this can be regarded as part of what you need as your partner or child's 'carer'. Many people who attend these supportive events keep in touch with each other, thus forming their own ongoing support group.

Summing Up

Counselling is a good way of getting emotional support and finding strategies that will help you to overcome specific problems.

Many people find the objective and empathetic support of a professional trained to listen immensely valuable. For those suffering stress, anxiety or depression, it can make the difference between feeling isolated and feeling supported.

Children of an AS Parent

10

Many adults with AS have children with their partners. If you are considering having children with your AS partner, you need to bear in mind that parenting children is a full-time, ongoing, challenging and exhausting job.

Many NT/AS couples make the decision not to have children. If this is you then it may be that you feel the added stress will be difficult to cope with.

You may think:

- If you have a child with an ASD that would mean additional problems for the NT parent already coping with an AS partner.

- A child would cause too much disruption, noise and chaos for the AS adult.

- You could not adjust your lives for a family.

Many couples do have children and any difficulties they may experience are not necessarily of greater severity than alternative or comparable difficulties experienced by other families. Their children may or may not have AS themselves.

While it is true that genetics plays a part and that many children who have AS have a parent or grandparent who also has the condition, what is the risk of an AS parent having a severely autistic child? Currently, according to the National Autistic Society, no generally accepted research or statistics exist. Severely autistic children can come from families previously unaffected by any kind of ASD, from families where there have been severely autistic children in the past or from families where there are already children or adults with the AS form of autism.

Non-AS children of AS parents

What effects could a parent with AS have on their non-AS child?

Negative:

- Shyness and lack of confidence in social situations which may be due to a combination of inherited AS traits or upbringing.

- Low self-esteem.

- A need for perfectionism.

- Various anxiety disorders such as OCD.

- Difficulty with developing their own identity or sense of self if this is not affirmed enough by the parent(s).

- A tendency to keep problems to themselves, a desire to please others, stress and depression later in life.

- Anxious attachment disorder. This is where a child's basic requirements of love, comfort and security are not met or are poorly met in the very early years and have long term if not life-long consequences for the child (see Oaasis website to download an information sheet on this subject – see help list).

Positive:

- Hard working.

- An understanding and tolerance of differences in others.

- An ability to adapt and develop self-help or compensatory techniques that will get them what they need.

- Independence.

- High intelligence and academic success – maybe inherited from the AS parent because intelligence is partly genetic or because an AS parent may be a good role model for hard work and may emphasise the importance of doing well academically.

As AS in adults has only really been diagnosed since the 1990s, it seems reasonable to assume that in decades past many AS adults would have married and produced children without any concerns. Those children would have grown up and any problems experienced might have been put down to having their parents' temperament/characteristics, not a disorder or the effects of being brought up by a parent with a disorder.

Today you might say we live in a slightly more enlightened age. Most parents realise that how they are and the type of person they are will have effects on their children. For all parents, these effects will be a mixture of good and not so good. But how can having AS have a negative effect on children and how can this be avoided?

Possible negative effects

- The AS parent may see their child in terms of what they achieve rather than who they are – resulting in damage to the child's sense of worth.

- The AS parent may be unaware that they need to provide emotional support and empathy – and be unable to do this.

- The AS parent may rarely use or remember to use emotional language that builds a child's self-esteem.

- The AS parent may leave the bulk of child rearing to their NT partner who becomes tired, stressed and unsupported. This in turn has a negative effect on the child.

Combating the negative

This is mostly a question of the NT parent compensating for the AS parent's shortcomings. If you are an NT parent, these important strategies will include:

- Telling your partner what kind of response your child needs and getting them to provide this.

- Ensuring that your partner does their share of parenting chores as far as possible.

- Having family times together when you talk about what you have been doing, how you feel and your thoughts about different things. This will teach your child that showing and sharing emotions is normal, good and helpful.

- Providing extra emotional support for your child.

- Encouraging your child to have friends.

- Enlisting the help and support of others who can provide emotional input for your child, e.g. grandparents, godparents, etc.

- Getting support for yourself.

Some research into the effects of children reared by AS parents tends to make discouraging reading. However, it is important to bear in mind that the writers of such research are basing their findings on families, parents and children experiencing great difficulties and not on all families where one parent has AS.

It's also important to remember that these troubled families are often contending with other issues. For example, many couples in second marriages where there are already children have problems. Someone with AS may find it difficult to understand their partner's bond with their children and may feel threatened by this.

However, where the AS parent is willing to develop his/her parenting skills and the NT parent is able to compensate for any lack of emotional input, is there any reason why the children will not have every chance of growing into well adjusted, confident young adults?

Bear in mind, also, that most AS adults who choose to have families are those who have responsible and well-respected jobs, are able to provide reliably for their families and do so with commitment and consistency. The secure base that this provides is also of importance to children.

Advice for the AS parent

It is important to remember that children are important for who they are and not just for what they achieve. If they don't feel that you view them in that way, this can be damaging to their self-esteem and to your relationship with them.

There may be some child rearing tasks that you are very good at and others you are not so good at. Some parents with AS find disciplining their children a problem and leave that to their NT partner, if they have one. This can result in an unfair burden being placed on the parent who takes all the initiative with discipline. Other AS parents can be too strict.

Parenting, however, is best done with support. It is a good idea to discuss any difficulties with your partner rather than just leaving the difficult bits to him/her. You both need to agree practices and support – and back each other up so that you are working as a team. That's the ideal though. If equal parenting or the strain of parenting is causing particular problems then it is a good idea to seek the advice and support of specialist counsellors who understand AS parents. They can help you avoid or limit the effects of problems. You might also find the following suggestions useful. They have all been made by parents who have AS or those whose partners have AS.

- If you know that both of you have AS then being aware of how to provide your child with the emotional input they need, and finding ways that you can both do this, is even more important.

- Go to parenting classes if you have them in your area and read parenting books.

- You may well love your child, but you also need to value and be interested in them for who they are, not for what they achieve.

> Where the AS parent is willing to develop his/her parenting skills and the NT parent is able to compensate for any lack of emotional input, is there any reason why the children will not have every chance of growing into well adjusted, confident young adults?

- Build your child's self-esteem by showing interest in their hobbies and spending time with them.

- Allow your child to be a child, i.e. let them be noisy, messy, invite friends round. Be aware that any sensory intolerances you have with regard to noise, disruption of routine, etc must not impose unfair rules on them.

- If you have more than one child, treat them the same – do not favour one over another.

- If your child experiences problems, you shouldn't assume they don't need your help if they don't ask. Unnatural though it may seem to you to do so, ask them how they are, how they feel and what you can do to help. If you have an NT partner, ask him/her what you could do to help.

- Once children reach adolescence then it is normal for problems to arise and for relationships to be strained as they strive to become independent.

- If the child is your step-child, remember it takes time to build a relationship with a step-child. Your partner's biological bond with his/her own children is natural. It is different and no threat to the bond your partner has with you.

- Don't act with indifference when your child experiences successes. Ask them about their experiences. Be pleased and supportive where appropriate. That's the job of parents too.

Summing Up

There is no such thing as the perfect parent. The majority of parents, whether they have AS or not, learn as they go, make mistakes and do the best job they can.

Having AS means that ways need to be found to ensure children receive the essential emotional input needed for normal development. When this happens children are able to grow up in a family where they are nurtured, loved and respected for who they are.

Glossary

Attachment disorder
The result of a child not receiving enough nurturing from its parent/carer, resulting in anxiety, low self-esteem, developmental or mental problems later in life.

Auditory discrimination
The ability to recognise differences in sounds and words, including sounds or words that are very similar.

Autoimmune
When a person's immune system attacks itself, this is called an autoimmune disease. Examples are diabetes, rheumatoid arthritis and multiple sclerosis. Some researchers believe ASDs can be due to an autoimmune reaction.

Autonomy
An individual's ability to determine and carry out their own actions in a way that is responsible and beneficial.

Biomedical
Related to the way our bodies process nutrients or whatever they are exposed to, and the way various toxins, diets, etc affect our mental and physical health.

Brain scanner
Equipment that is able to scan or read the way a person's brain or part of their brain is working.

Cognition
Learning, thinking and problem solving processes in the brain.

Co-morbid condition
A condition a person suffers from alongside or in addition to the main one, e.g. someone who has AS might also have dyslexia.

Diagnostician
Person qualified to diagnose a condition or conditions, e.g. a doctor, psychiatrist, etc.

Dyslexia
A learning difficulty mainly connected with reading, writing and spelling.

Dyspraxia
A motor or movement co-ordination disability.

Echolalia
A habit of, or need to, repeat a sound or words just heard.

Emotional deprivation
A condition suffered by those who do not receive enough affirmation, attention or support from a key person or from others. This can result in the person developing anxiety, depression or low self-esteem.

Genetics
The study of hereditary conditions or features and how these are passed from parents to their children.

Human Genome Project

A research project that attempts to study and understand all human genes and human origins.

Impairment

A damaged or weakened ability in a particular area.

Mindblindness

The inability to work out what someone means through non-verbal clues or behaviour.

Neurodevelopment

The way the brain and nervous system has developed in a person. Those with ASDs are thought to have differences in the way parts of their brains have developed. This means that those parts work differently.

Neurology/neurological

Refers to the way the brain and nervous system works. A neurological disorder means one that is caused by the brain or nervous system working in a way that is not normal.

Neuro typical (NT)

A person whose brain patterns/behaviours are considered normal.

Normalise

Adjusting something to make it acceptable or normal.

Obsessive compulsive disorder (OCD)

An anxiety disorder in which sufferers have constant unwelcome intrusive thoughts and perform behaviours to relieve themselves of these, e.g. constant handwashing.

Paediatrician

A qualified medical doctor who has specialised in treating children.

Pedantic

The strict insistence that what is said is exactly or literally correct.

Prevalence

The extent to which something exists or is found.

Prosody

The rhythm of speech. Some people with AS speak in a very flat tone.

Psychopathy

Immoral and/or antisocial behaviour that stems from a form of mental illness.

Reciprocity/reciprocal

The ability to give back to the same degree as you receive, e.g. the to and fro of conversation, or the returning of a suitable action or gesture when you have received one.

Relational disorder

A disability that is mainly obvious when the person who suffers from it tries to relate to others. This is because the person finds understanding another's point of view difficult, or finds socially acceptable behaviours confusing or difficult to understand.

Ritualistic behaviour

This can be always wanting to do something a certain way or insisting that certain things are always a certain way. An example for someone with AS may be wanting to go through a certain routine in the same order before leaving for work each morning.

Stimming

A self-stimulatory repetitive action that comforts the person performing it, e.g., repetitive throat clearing, over-blinking, tapping feet or fingers.

Tourette's syndrome

A neurological disorder that causes uncontrollable tics. They may be physical (e.g. jerking the head or throwing an arm up in the air) or verbal (e.g. shouting out a particular word, maybe swearing).

Help List

The AQ Test

Address: Autism Research Centre, Section of Developmental Psychiatry, University of Cambridge, Douglas House, 18b Trumpington Road, Cambridge, CB2 8AH

Tel: 01223 746057 | Email: admin@autismresearchcentre.com

Website: http://aspergerstest.net/aq-test/

Info: The AQ test is 50 questions from psychologist Simon Baron-Cohen at Cambridge Autism Research Centre. The test can indicate whether a person may be on the ASD spectrum.

Asperger Syndrome Website

Website: www.asperger-syndrome.me.uk

Info: Website created by someone who has personal experience of the condition with many pages of information.

Asperger's Syndrome Foundation

Address: The Asperger's Syndrome Foundation c/o Littlestone Golding, Eden House, Reynolds Road, Beaconsfield, HP9 2FL

Email: info@aspergerfoundation.org.uk

Website: http://www.aspergerfoundation.org.uk/

Info: Awareness and information for those affected by AS.

Autism Alliance

www.autism-alliance.org.uk

Info: Major UK network of specialist autism charities.

Autism Research Institute

Address: Autism Research Institute, 4182 Adams Avenue, San Diego, CA, 92116

Tel: (+141)866-366-3361 | Email: director@autism.com

Website: www.autism.com

Info: Includes information about biomedical interventions for autism.

British Psychoanalytic Council (BPC)

Address: British Psychoanalytic Council, Suite 7, 19-23 Wedmore Street, London N19 4RU

Tel: 020 7561 9240 | Email: mail@bpc.org.uk

Website: https://www.bpc.org.uk/

Info: Information, news and debate about psychoanalytic and other therapies. Therapist directory.

CAT Kit

Address: c/o Future Horizons, Inc. 721 W. Abram St. Arlington TX 76013
Tel: (+141) 817-277-0727
Website: www.cat-kit.com
Info: A method to teach and explore feelings, communication skills, behaviour and social skills for autistic and non-autistic children. Devised with the help of Tony Attwood, asperger/autism expert. Can be used by parents, teachers or counsellors and for small group or individual use.

Hendrickx Associates

Address: 2 Myrtle Road, Lancing, West Sussex BN15 9HX
Tel: 07803 325542 | Email: info@asperger-training.com
Website: www.asperger-training.com
Info: Based in West Sussex. Provides training, counselling, workshops for those with AS, their families and professionals. Sarah Hendrickx and her AS partner, Keith Newton, are authors of Asperger Syndrome – A Love Story. Sarah Hendrickx is also the author of other titles about AS – see book list for details.

Maxine Aston

Website: www.maxineaston.co.uk
Info: Website of counsellor, Asperger expert and author of books about living with AS. Has details of counselling, training and workshops for partners of those who live with someone with AS.

National Autistic Society

England and Head Office address: 393 City Road, London, EC1V 1NG
Tel: 0808 800 4104 (helpline) | Email: nas@nas.org.uk
Cymru (Wales) address: 6-7 Village Way, Greenmeadow Springs Business Park, Tongwynlais, Cardiff, CF15 7NE
Tel: 02920 629 312 | Email: wales@nas.org.uk
Scotland address: Central Chambers, 1st Floor, 109 Hope Street, Glasgow, G2 6LL
Tel: 0141 221 8090 | Email: scotland@nas.org.uk
Northern Ireland address: 59 Malone Road, Belfast, BT9 6SA
Tel: 02890 687 066 | Email: northern.ireland@nas.org.uk
Website: www.autism.org.uk
Info: Leading UK charity with branches in Scotland, Northern Ireland, Wales and England. Promotes awareness and knowledge of ASDs. This charity's vast and in-depth website gives details of just about every issue that affects the person with ASD and their family as well as professionals, employers and teachers.

They offer programmes that support children and their families. They also run training schemes that help young people with finding training and work. Their membership magazine is *My Autism Magazine*.

Oxford Autism Research Group

Address: University Department of Psychiatry, Warneford Hospital, Oxford, OX3 7JX
Tel: 01865 618200 | Email: information@psych.ox.ac.uk
Website: https://www.psych.ox.ac.uk/research/autism
Info: Current research and information about autism and Asperger's syndrome, including information on the MEG scanner. Website includes useful links for professionals and families.

Play and Language for Autistic Youngsters (PLAY)

Address: 3031 Miller Road, Ann Arbor, Michigan, 48103
Tel: (+141) 734-585-5333
Email: contact form available at http://www.playproject.org/contact/
Website: www.playproject.org
Info: A therapy intervention programme to show parents how to help their children play and become more socially interactive.

Social Stories TM

Address: P.O. Box 1007, Jenison, MI 49429-1007 U.S.A.
Email: carol@carolgraysocialstories.com
Website: http://carolgraysocialstories.com
Info: Invented by Carol Gray in the 1990s. Advice on how to write Social Stories TM, downloadable stories and other useful resources and links are available from the official website above.

Tony Attwood

Address: The Asperger's Syndrome Clinic, PO Box 224, Petrie, Queensland, 4502 Australia
Tel: +61 (0)7 3285 7888 | Email: tony@tonyattwood.com.au
Website: www.tonyattwood.com.au
Info: Informative website of clinical psychologist, author and world-renowned leading autism expert.

UK Association for Humanistic Psychology Practitioners

(UKAHPP)

Address: BCM AHPP, London, WC1N 3XX

Tel: 08457 660326 (answerphone) | Email: admin@ahpp.org.uk

Website: www.ahpp.org

Info: Organisation for all those who apply the theories of humanistic psychology in their work. Includes guide to humanistic psychology and a searchable directory of members.

UK Council for Psychotherapy (UKCP)

2nd Floor Edward House, 2 Wakley Street, London, EC1V 7LT

Tel: 020 7014 9955 | Email: info@ukcp.org.uk

Website: http://www.ukcp.org.uk

Info: Register of qualified and registered counsellors/therapists.

Book List

Adolescents on the Autism Spectrum
Sicile-Kira, C. (Penguin Books, New York, 2006)

Alone Together: Making an Asperger Marriage Work
Bentley, K. (Jessica Kingsley Publishers, London, 2007)

Approaches to Autism: An Easy to Use Guide to Many and Varied Approaches to Autism
(The National Autistic Society, London, revised 2007)

The Asperger Children's Toolkit
Musgrave, F. (Jessica Kingsley Publishers, London, 2012)

The Asperger Couple's Workbook, Practical Advice and Activities for Couples and Counsellors
Aston, M. (Jessica Kingsley Publishers, London, 2008)

Asperger's Rules!: How To Make Sense of School and Friends
Grossberg, B. (Magination Press, London, 2012)

Asperger Syndrome and Employment: What People with Asperger Syndrome Really Really Want
Hendrickx, S. (Jessica Kingsley Publishers, London, 2009)

Can I Tell You About Asperger's Syndrome? A Guide for Friends and Family
Welton, J. (Jessica Kingsley Publishers, London, 2003)

The Complete Guide to Asperger's Syndrome
Attwood, T. (Jessica Kingsley Publishers, London, 2006)

The Diagnostic and Statistical Manual of Mental Disorders (DSM-V)
(American Psychiatric Association, 5th edition, 2013, Washington DC)
Official manual outlining diagnosable mental and neurological conditions.

How to Make School Make Sense: A Parents' Guide to Helping the Child with Asperger Syndrome
Lawrence, C. (Jessica Kingsley Publishers, London, 2008)

I Have Aspergers
Clemens, E. (lulu.com, London, 2014)

The International Classification of Diseases (ICD-10)
(10th edition, 1992, World Health Organisation)

Mindblindness: An Essay on Autism and Theory of Mind
Baron-Cohen, S. (The MIT Press, USA, 1997)

The Red Beast: Controlling Anger in Children with Asperger's Syndrome
Al-Ghani, K. I. (Jessica Kingsley Publishers, London, 2008)

Why Love Matters: How Affection Shapes a Baby's Brain
Sue Gerhardt, Routledge; (2nd edition, Routledge, 2014)

Sources of Further Information

Frith, Uta, 'Mindblindness and the brain in autism', Neuron, Vol 32, Issue 6.

Miles, Brenda and Simpson, Richard L, 'Effective Practices for Students with Asperger Syndrome, Focus on Exceptional Children', Personal Communication, 4 June 1997.

Ownby, Melissa Hincha – search under name, March 2008. Covers diagnostic tools used in ASD diagnosis.

'Relative Success for Autism', gene hunt article, www.labonline.com

Silberman, Steve, 'The Geek Syndrome', Wired, www.wired.com

Smith, Garnder and Bowler, 'Deficits in Free Recall', NCBI publications. March 2007. An article about research into the differences in the way those with AS learn and recall compared to those without AS.

Walsh, Dr Christopher – search under name or: sfari.org/news/Christopher-walsh-solving-mysteries-of-the-mind-in-the-middle-east Genetic research and gene therapy.

'Understanding and Treating Autistic Behaviours', Part 1 Non-pharmacologic Therapy, Vol No 32:11. May be available online or search under article title, www.uspharmacist.com/content/paediatrics

Your Autism Magazine, National Autistic Society members' publication. Up-to-date information on research, interventions, education and publications.